How to Know God's Will in Any Situation

Nassera Victoria

ISBN: 978-29558275-0-5

CONTENTS

How to know God's Will in Any Situation

Nassera Victoria

INTRODUCTION

What is God's will in this situation? What am I supposed to do in these circumstances? What decision should I make? What attitude am I supposed to adopt in this situation? All of us have these questions at least once in a while. We sometimes face such situations that challenge us to find appropriate answers while seeking God's will.

Each situation, each circumstance, each trial is different and takes on a unique aspect. This is why we cannot respond to each similar situation the same way. We have to find, for each situation, the appropriate and unique way to respond.

If we want to respond to each situation, circumstance, and trial in the appropriate way according to God's will, we need first to know Him and His ways.

This book presents the main ways of God, as mentioned in the Scriptures.

The Bible invites us to seek God's ways and not our own ways. I believe that in order to be trained to respond according to God's will to each and every situation, it is key to understand God's ways. Understanding God's ways is the same thing as understanding Him. His ways are His ways of operating and His ways of being.

"In all your ways, acknowledge Him, and He shall direct your paths." **Proverbs 3:6**

*"And now Israel, what does The Lord your God require of you, but to fear The Lord your God, **to walk in all His ways**, and to love Him..."* **Deuteronomy 10:12**

Those two verses highlight the fact that God expects us to choose His ways rather than our ways in each situation. His ways are supposed to become our ways.

4

He promises us that if we seek His ways, which means that we seek to walk in His ways, He will direct our paths. Therefore, in order to respond according to God's will in each situation, seeking and choosing His ways rather than ours represents an essential key in our Christian life.

What are His ways? What is the difference between our ways and His ways? How can we acknowledge Him in all our ways? How can we know His will in every situation? The purpose of this book is to answer those questions and help anyone who wants to better know God and gain a deeper understanding of His ways in order to hear God's voice and discern His will.

Above all, this book is an invitation to seek Him and to seek to know Him like never before. Many know a lot of things about God from what they have heard and read through the years, but only a few really know God.

I hope that speaking about the ways of God as they have been revealed to me through meditation on the Scriptures, as well as through my experiences with Him, will communicate a passion to know Him.

To know Him changes everything. And even trying to act according to His will without knowing Him would be legalism. This is why more than anything else—more than presenting some keys on how to discern His will in every situation while presenting His ways—my purpose is to present God as the source of all joy and contentment, of all power, knowledge and peace, with the hope to ignite or renew a passion to know Him and seek Him.

I- WHAT ARE GOD'S WAYS?

As Christians, we often speak or hear about God's ways. We know we are supposed to follow God's ways, and we all have a general idea of what it means. But do we exactly know what it represents and what it looks like to follow God's ways? What does it truly mean? What do the ways of God include and look like? What are the ways of God?

In this book, we identify seven ways of God we are called to walk in, which gather the main characteristics of God's nature, His character, His attributes and what He likes. The ways of God we are called to walk in are a reflection of who God is and what pleases Him. We will see that what pleases

Him is actually always in correlation to His love for us.

What is a way?

The term "ways" is abundantly used in the Bible to describe conducts, attitudes, works, and hearts of men. It generally means the actions of men and the way they do them, as well as motivations of the heart.

The Bible defines God's ways as different from men's ways. Everything that refers to God, His word, all that He does, the way He does it, and His heart, as well as the council He gives to men to follow – all these together represent His ways. God's wish and heart for us is to follow His ways, as He knows our life, happiness and prosperity depends on it.

His ways are higher and greater than ours, and as children of God our destiny is to walk in the ways of He who has created us. Our destiny is to follow the path of life that He has drawn for our lives.

By "ways" in the Bible, we must understand:

Conduct

The word "ways" in the Bible mainly represents the conduct of men. It includes decisions, choices, actions, attitudes, intentions of the heart and motivations. The ways we walk in represent our whole conduct in life. This is the main definition we must understand from the term "ways" in the Bible.

Works

Our ways include works and actions. A lot of verses in the Scriptures contain the word "ways" to mean "what we do". The expression of "walking in His ways" is often associated with obeying God's commandments, and therefore doing what He wants.

Heart's attitude and character

But "God's ways" in the Bible doesn't only mean our works and actions. We can do His works and not walk in His ways. This is what Jesus talks about in **Matthew 7: 22-23**:

Matthew 7:22-23 *"Many will say to Me in that day, Lord, Lord, have we not prophesied in your Name, cast out demons in your Name, and done many wonders in your Name. And then, I will declare to them: I never knew you, depart from Me, you who practice lawlessness."*

We clearly see here the difference in doing His works, but

not His will. Walking in lawlessness while doing what seems to be God's work is not walking in His ways. We can do works that seem to be His works but do them because of wrong motivations, rebellion, pride, or legalism. All these things are more heart attitudes and also represent our ways according to the biblical thought. Our ways include heart attitudes and character.

Motivations of the heart

The source of any of our actions comes from our heart. Depending on how we feed our heart and what we feed it with, our motivations can be right or wrong according to God. God searches the depths of our hearts, and our ways involve the intentions and motivations of our heart.

God is never impressed by the works and actions of men. He searches our depths, our hearts, and this is actually what He looks at first.

Proverbs 16:2 *"All the ways of a man are pure in his own eyes, but The Lord weighs the spirits."*

Our ways, therefore, include motivations and intentions of

the heart. This aspect is taken into account each time "our ways" is spoken about in the Bible.

The word "ways" in the Bible refers to two main aspects: our conduct, actions, works, and behavior; and our character and our heart's attitudes and motivations. We can then summarize them as: what we do, how we do it, and why we do it.

What are God's ways?

God's ways mentioned in the Bible always refer to: the Word of God, His thought, His commandments, His will, Who He is, His character and heart. As His children and His people, we are destined to walk according to who God is, what He says and His will. We are supposed to walk in His ways, and not our own ways. His Word, His council, His thought, His character, His works, all represent His ways and are what we are supposed to follow. We notice that His ways include both what concerns obedience in actions, conduct, and works as well as the imitation of His character.

In this book we present the seven main ways of God, in

which we can find the main attributes of God.

What is the difference between our ways and His ways?

Isaiah 55: 8-9 *"For my thoughts are not your thoughts, nor are your ways my ways, says The Lord. For as the heavens are higher than the earth, so are my ways higher than your ways, and my thoughts than your thoughts."*

God is the Creator of everything. He is Sovereign upon everything. He knows everything, can do everything, and sees everything. He has a whole plan of love for mankind, and His heart's desire is to see all men saved so that they can live in eternal communion of love with Him. His precepts, His word, and His council are always to instruct us in truth, make us free in knowing Him, perfect us to His own image, and prepare us to rule with Him in eternity.

His ways represent the model for us to follow. He is God above all things, and He has created us in His image, to be like Him. We are destined to seek to live in His likeness. In our character, nature, conduct and works, we are supposed to imitate Him.

As we are His children, He is the one who seeks our good,

who acts for our good, who watches over us and protects us. He is the one who instructs us and perfects us to be how we are meant to be in this earth and in heaven.

Therefore, all His ways are the model for us to follow as He is our model, our Father.

THE WAYS OF GOD

In God's Kingdom, there is one main way that is at the source of any activity, any decision, any movement. This way is at the source of all the other ways in the Kingdom of God, and if we choose to walk in it, it empowers us and helps us to walk in all the other ways of God.

This main way is Love.

Love is not only a way of walking for God. It is His very nature. It is the way He is, the way He thinks, the way He feels. In all what He does, Love is the first and very motivation. He is Love.

If we understand, if we taste that God is Love, we understand who He is.

As God is Love and we are His children, we are supposed to be like Him. Not only to walk in love, but to be love. Love is supposed to become our very nature as well.

Love implies other ways that we will focus on later.

1 WAY OF LOVE

Above everything, God is Love. God loves us. He delights in us. He created the whole universe, the Earth and all that it contains, for us to enjoy it. He created men to take care of Eden, the garden of His delights, not as a simple guardian, but as the delight of His delights. God was enjoying Himself in seeing how Adam would name the elements He had created, exactly as a father enjoys himself observing his children growing in a new sphere of maturity. That is actually it: we are His children and we are the center of His attention and of His care. He calls us the apple of His eyes, His special treasure, and the flock of His pasture.

He so loved us that He gave His Son for the redemption and salvation of anyone who would receive Him as Lord and Savior. He offered the perfect lamb who takes away the sin of the world; His Son who is one with Him, who "being the brightness of His Glory, and the express image of His

Person."

God says, "I am". He is. He is what? He is Love. It also means that He is Love eternally, because He always will be. He will never cease to be; therefore, He will never cease to be Love.

Love is powerful. There is nothing more powerful than love. Love is *"as strong as death"* (Song of Solomon 8: 6). Nothing can resist love.

About love

What is love? Some would say it is a feeling, some would say it is more of a decision. We all have an intuitive comprehension of what love is, which makes us generally understand one another on this subject. We recognize love when we see it, when it is manifested to us, or when we manifest it toward others. We recognize it when we experience it.

God IS Love.

Through this statement, we can then draw a definition that everyone would agree on: we know that God is Love and that He came on Earth to offer the sacrifice of His own life to

16

save us; therefore, we can summarize the definition of love as being a gift of oneself. Love, then, is the act of giving oneself to others. There are many ways to give oneself to others, but love, at least, is the action of giving a part of what we have, we are, or what we do to others.

The Bible says that "*God has so loved the world that He gave His only begotten Son, that whoever believes in Him should not perish but have everlasting life.*" (John 3:16). This verse teaches us a lot about love. It is said that because God so loved the word, He gave His only Son. It means that His love was first, and His gift came because of His love. His gift was a manifestation of His love, but love was first. We can conclude that love doesn't consist of action only, but is an intention of the heart, a feeling or an emotion first. Love is not only a feeling or an emotion (because God manifested His love through His amazing gift), and it is not only an isolated action, but love is an activity of the heart (feeling, passion, compassion, etc...) that compels a person into action.

1 Corinthians 13:4-8 "*Love is patient, love is kind. It does not envy, it does not boast, it is not proud. It does not dishonor others, it is not self-seeking, it is not easily* *angered. It keeps no record of wrongs. Love does not delight in evil but rejoices with the truth. It always protects, always trusts, always hopes, always perseveres. Love never fails."*

It is interesting to notice that most characteristics of love mentioned in this verse refer to character. Love is first a character, a form of heart, a nature.

In this definition given by Paul of what love looks like, we see that every one of its aspects is actually a fruit of the Spirit. Patience, kindness, humility, peace, truth, goodness, and perseverance are all the fruits of the Spirit mentioned in Galatians 5:22. Love itself is listed first as one of them. If all that composes love are fruits of the Spirit, Love is the most complete fruit of the Spirit. It includes in itself all the other fruits of the Holy Spirit. Therefore, Love is the ultimate or the most complete expression of the Spirit of God. It is not surprising as God is love.

We know that the fruits of the Spirit come out from our walk by the Holy Spirit. Paul says in **Galatians 5:** *"So I say: walk by the Spirit, and you will not gratify the desires of the flesh,"* and, *"Since we live by the Spirit, let us keep in step with*

The Spirit." The walk is not only living by the Spirit but also manifesting the Spirit. Or being able to manifest the Spirit implies being in constant communion with Him.

To be in a continual communion with God is the condition sine qua non to manifest His Spirit. This is also why Paul exhorted to "pray continually." It is possible to manifest the fruits of the Spirit for a while, and months or years later, to walk by the flesh if we let our communion with God become interrupted or weakened. From our continual relationship with God can only flow the expression of who He is: Love.

If the manifestation of love is patience, kindness, humility, peace, truth, goodness and perseverance all together, then growing in love also helps us develop in those areas. Love is the best mainspring to develop other fruits of the Spirit such as those. Because we love, we become patient, kind, perseverant, etc. with the people we love. Therefore, love should be the first thing to pursue.

The first and second commandment of the law is, "You shall love The Lord your God with all your heart, with all your soul, with all your strength and with all your mind; and your neighbor as yourself." Jesus said that all the law is accomplished in those two commandments. It means that to truly love God above all, and our neighbor as ourselves, is the main way in God's Kingdom.

As sons and daughters of God who is Love, we are called first to be love like Him and love Him first who gave us everything. He must be the subject of our adoration, and only in that condition can He empower us with His love to love others.

We come to Him, and He fills us with His love. We love Him, and then we are able to love others like He loves them. To love others like He does, we continually need to come to His arms of love to fill us and renew us.

God's love has nothing to do with human love. It's a deep and unconditional love. Men's love is superficial, based on affinities, character, personal history, appearance etc., but God's love is full, whole, deep, faithful, and everlasting. This is this godly love we are meant to be filled with.

Everything in the kingdom of God comes out of the Love of the Father. It is the source of everything. Just as everything that God does comes out from His love, we, as sons and daughters, are supposed to be led and motivated by His love in all that we do.

But we cannot do anything in the kingdom that will be fruitful without first receiving His love and loving Him.

How does it look like to love God?

God loved us first, and the only thing we can offer Him is our love and thankfulness. How can we love God?

To know Him

First, we cannot love God if we don't know Him. We love Him when we know Him. There are several levels in knowing God.

When I first accepted Jesus, I didn't know Him. I just met Him through a revelation. I didn't grow up in a Christian family. I was wondering about the existence of God and about the meaning of life when I decided one day to address those words to God: "God, if you do exist, you must be able to speak, then speak to me; I want to know who you are." I spoke those words from the very bottom of my heart, and was sincerely opened to receive any response from Him. I would have definitely come to the conclusion that God doesn't exist if He wouldn't have revealed Himself to me.

This is what happened: several days or weeks later, I was just standing and thinking in front of the window when suddenly I physically felt something like a strength coming from above to me, like a weight of laundry falling to my shoulders; and immediately my eyes closed and I couldn't open them anymore. Then I heard a very clear voice coming from the inside of me, but it was obvious that it was not my own thought. This voice said, "I have some plans for you, but you have to decide to follow me." From that moment on, I knew that God existed and that He had just spoken to me.

The next day, I was led to read the Gospels in the Bible that I already had at home. When I started to read, I had the irrepressible conviction that this Jesus of the Bible was the one who had spoken to me the day before. I never stopped reading the Scriptures and following Him since.

My point is that at that moment I didn't know God, when I came to Him and decided to follow Him. I just met Him and only knew He was God and Had spoken to me. This is the very first level of knowing Him. Knowing His existence. But then, one has to get to know Him, and to continue to seek to know Him.

There are two main ways that lead us to know God: to know

His word, and to spend some time with Him in prayer.

To know His word

The more we grow in the comprehension and the meditation of the scriptures, the more we know Him. There is always more to learn and to know about Him in the scriptures. In reading the Bible, we not only learn things from God and about Him but also we really get to know Him. Through all the Bible, God manifests His redeeming heart for men and His passion for His people. Among many, one passage in the Bible that reflects very well the passion of God for His people is the Lamentations of Jeremiah. Through Jeremiah's prophetic words, God spreads out His heart, His cry for His people who continually rejected Him after He had demonstrated to them such faithfulness, power and love to deliver them from their oppressions.

Also, reading and meditating on the Word of God helps us to know God better, not only through what we discover of Him but also because this is the living Word that opens our minds and generates faith and love in us. Reading and meditating on the Word of God positions our spirit to receive His thought and His mind so that we can know Him. It connects us directly with Him through our heart that receives it.

To know Him in Person

We have direct access to God, through Jesus's sacrifice at the cross for us. He tore the veil that was separating us from The Father because of sin. God is a real person who speaks not only through His written word, and we can know Him by spending some time in His presence.

Setting some time apart to communicate with God, to let Him speak to us, touch us, and minister to us while meditating on the Scriptures, is the main way of getting to know God. As I mentioned earlier, getting to know God is a lifelong process; we will always discover some news aspects of Him, and His Glory is limitless. We can always grow in getting to know Him. The more I spend time with Him, the more I know Him. The way He speaks to me, the way He operates in me, the way He thinks, and the way He loves me makes me know Him. I can experience His tangible presence with its characteristics: peace, joy, love, kindness, holiness, power, glory... and I also discover His personality through what He likes and what He likes to do.

The more I spend time with Him, the more I know Him. Communion with God is the same as communion with someone we love; after years of communion with a person we love (husband, wife, friend, etc.), we know what the other person is thinking just by looking in his or her eyes. It is the same with God; we discern His thinking because of the years of communion.

Communion with God can take on different aspects: prayer, worship, intercession, soaking, meditating on the scripture, etc. The list here is not exhaustive. We can be in the presence of God just by being silent and waiting on Him to speak to us. Prayer is the generic word for all those kinds of communications with God. Prayer doesn't necessarily mean to ask for something. To pray simply means to communicate with God.

Several times, Jesus told the disciples about the way of praying. He gave two main principles about prayer: the first one is being consistent and perseverant in prayer. As the Scriptures say, "He who asks, receives," and, "Ask and you will receive." He also gave the parable of the widow and the judge, in which the judge finally decides to intervene for the widow not because of his righteousness, but just because of her consistent begging to him. Paul also exhorts us in Colossians to pray uninterruptedly.

The second principle about prayer that Jesus gave is not to

use vain repetitions or long speeches. The fulfillment of prayer doesn't come from the length or the volume of our prayer, but simply because of His grace. God always looks at the heart and He is never impressed by appearance or the form of things.

This second principle of prayer shows us how God prefers us to be in sincere communion with Him, rather than to be in a recitation mode. He wants us to be real with Him, as it is said in Hebrews. He knows exactly where we are at, and He doesn't need us to play a role.

Real communion then always variates in different kinds of expressions: confession, thankfulness, supplication, worship, adoration, expressions of love, declarations, silence, etc.

The reason why God wants us to be real with Him is first because it demonstrates our faith toward Him, in that He is our Father, the one who sent His own Son to pay the price for our redemption, justification and reconciliation, and who gave us access to the Throne of the Grace of God, the one we truly trust to forgive us. The second reason is because He wants our hearts and not our sacrifices. He is in a true relationship with us, in which He gave everything to us and shares all His glory with us, and He longs after our hearts.

The Lord can also appear to us in visions or open visions, and we can live some real experiences with Him. This can also be a part of knowing Him and seeing what He likes and what He likes to do. For example, I saw Jesus several times in a garden and enjoying flowers. I saw Him dance in a garden several times. I realized then that He liked gardens and flowers, and He likes to dance.

Spending some time with God will always lead us to know Him more, and knowing Him more will always lead us to love Him more. The more I know Him, the more I love Him.

In His presence, we can receive His Love. Let Him comfort us, renew us, and fill us with His love and peace. Because of His love, we are able to love Him.

Worship

"God demonstrates His own love toward us, in that while we were still sinners, Christ died for us." **Romans 5:8**.

God loved us first, and one of the main things we can offer Him is our thankfulness and worship. We have not much to offer Him but our love, and one of the expressions of our love toward Him is worship. Worship is an expression of our love for God. From abundance of heart, the mouth speaks. Just as when we are in love we cannot help but speak about the person we love and tell this person's praises, our passion for God automatically generates praises and worship to Him. It is difficult to imagine someone who would love God but who would not praise and worship Him. Worship celebrates God. It is also an expression of our thankfulness. The psalms invite us in a large measure to worship and praise God in all times, and everywhere.

Also, worship allows us to focus on God, and not on our own condition.

Focusing on the beauty, the majesty, the sovereignty of God confirms our faith and the fact that our attention and expectations are in Him.

Worshipping God is not only a sincere declaration of praises but also it touches every area of our lives: our behavior with people, how we respect and honor God's people and God's creation, the way we take care of ourselves, our health, our body, the way we raise our children, how we steward finances, etc.

Every aspect of our lives should glorify God, and in any of our decision we have an opportunity to manifest our love to

God.

Faith

Faith is an attribute that pleases God. We cannot please Him without faith. We can show Him our love in showing Him our faith. As a father, He loves to see His children rely on Him and depend on Him. The manifestation of our faith is a demonstration of our love for God because we show Him we trust Him, we believe Him, and we accept His intervention, leading and provision. We place ourselves under His Sovereignty, His Fathership, which is the real humility, and our faith is a response to His Love.

Faith is really what God expects from us. He wants us to trust Him, above all, often against what we can see with natural sight. This is true faith when in the middle of the darkest opposition and circumstances, we continue to believe what He said and promised.

Through faith, we submit our own will to His will and accept Him to rule over our lives. Our communion with God is a love and faith story. We receive everything from Him by faith: His salvation, His protection, His love, His equipment to serve others, His anointing, His direction, etc.

This is why faith is directly correlated to our love for Him: we cannot love Him if we don't have faith and we cannot believe Him if we don't love Him.

Faith and love work together and the more I love Him, the more I trust Him. The more I grow in the knowledge of who He is, the more I am amazed by His faithfulness and stillness and love, and the more I trust Him.

Works

Works are one of the most concrete ways of showing God that we love Him. In practicing our faith by works according to His will, we confirm our obedience and belonging to Him. Faith without works is dead. Faith is demonstrated by the works, and works demonstrate whom we follow, whom we trust, and whom we love.

Not all works reveal our obedience and love to God, though, but only those that are initiated by the Holy Spirit. Many works can seem build the kingdom of God, or can look like things that can be pleasing to God but have nothing to do with His will. Only the works that are motivated by Him and by His love are the real works He expects of us.

When we speak about works concerning the Kingdom of God, we generally think about doing things to build the Kingdom of God, like feeding the poor, serving the Saints, preaching the Gospel, etc. Those works are indeed what God expects from His people generally, but we are supposed to do the works He leads us to do personally, being incorporated in the body of Christ who is meant to be the complete expression of who He is on Earth.

When it comes to the works in the Bible, we see that they are more generally things that we do relating to our faith and our relationship with God. For example, in Hebrews, when Paul is listing the works of faith of the great men of faith in history: like when Abraham obeyed God in bringing Isaac to be sacrificed. Most of time, God will ask simple acts of obedience from us. Those simple acts of obedience in our lives are counted as works according to God. These are the works in which we manifest our obedience and love to God.

To love others

The second commandment is to "love your neighbor as yourself". The main way in God's kingdom is love. Loving God compels us to love others. Loving others is the most obvious sign of our love for God. Jesus said that it is because of the love we have for each other that the world will know that we are His disciples.

1 John 4:12 "*If we love one another, God abides in us, and*

His love has been perfected in us." Our love for others testifies that we are in God, that we receive His love and that we respond to His love.

What does it look like to love others?

God expects us to walk in Love like Him. To love others like ourselves. **Romans 13:10** *"Love is the fulfillment of the law."*

Every Christian sincerely wants to love others, but often faces some obstacles in pursuing love for others. Among these obstacles, we can find: differences, offenses, incomprehension, miscommunication, judgment, etc. In pursuing love, we have to be willing to confront those obstacles.

First, if we have to pursue love, it's because Earth is inhabited by sin and sin works against life and love. When God created men, it is said that He created men in His image. Therefore, we were meant to be love like Him from the beginning. But because of sin, men separated themselves from God and weren't one with Him anymore, with His Spirit and His heart. The consequence of that is that men are not able to manifest God's love anymore, unless they are reconciled with Him through Jesus Christ.

The only possibility of loving like God is to have continual communion with Him and to let Him rule in us.

There are three kinds of love.

The Bible speaks about a natural affection; this is the first kind of love. It is said that in the end of time, men will be without natural affection. This kind of love is simply love that comes from the heart of men. Love for our family members, for our friends is generally natural affection. This love can be very strong and can produce good things, but it can also be easily affected because of the nature of men's heart itself, which is sin. It is a limited and fragile love.

The second kind of love is love that comes from God's heart and flows in us for others. This love is completely different; it is wider, deeper, stronger, and higher. It doesn't require any effort. We feel we are completely in alignment with God's heart. This love compels us to action for others: prayer, intercession, service, gifts, help, exhortation, encouragement, much grace when they disappoint us, etc.

If we receive God's love, His love enables us to love others as He loves them. His Spirit empowers us to see as He sees and feel as He feels. This ability to love can take on various forms, but it is operated through the movement of

33

the Holy Spirit in us.

There is a third kind of love that consists of a decision and simple obedience to God. When love becomes a challenge, most of time we have to position ourselves to be obedient to God and choose to love rather than to judge or contest. We often have to choose between egocentrism or surrendering to God to let love being manifested. This is then a decision we make. This kind of love is often practical love, obedience, righteousness, and... effort.

Here are some key principles that can help us to walk in love successfully.

1- Love is often a decision.

Paul in Corinthians exhorts us to pursue love. To pursue implies to make efforts and make decisions that are sometimes against our own human nature.

There are many kinds of situations in the relational area in which we have to pursue love by decision. Depending on what kind of obstacles to love we are facing in a situation, the decisions can vary. In some situations of offense, damages, and transgression, we need to forgive. Forgiveness is a decision.

Forgiveness

Forgiveness is a bridge between both riversides of a broken relationship. It allows the relationship to go on without the infection of bitterness or anger. It is a pass that enables love to continue to flow. Forgiveness is a powerful weapon of love. It also contains in itself the power of setting us free from any bondage related to bitterness or anger like diseases, blocked situations caused by unforgiveness, fear, etc.

As a Christian, it is not an option, but God warns us that if we don't forgive, we won't be forgiven. We don't have to base forgiveness on what we feel, as forgiveness is more of a juridical status: we decide, we pronounce it, and it is done.

In situations in which we have to face difference, disagreement or misunderstanding, we need to compromise to find a common ground of agreement, to keep the bond of peace.

The bond of peace

Ephesians 4:1-3 "*I therefore the prisoner in the Lord, beseech you to walk worthy of the calling you were called,* *with all lowliness and gentleness, with longsuffering, bearing in one another in love, endeavoring to keep the unity of the Spirit in the bond of peace."*

In this verse, we clearly see how love is associated to endeavors to keep unity by peace. To pursue peace is a condition sine qua non to love. A question to ask ourselves in a situation of disagreement is: what can I personally do to keep a bond of peace, to remain in unity with the people involved?

How do I pursue love?

In some challenging relational situations, an essential question to ask ourselves is: what is best in the situation – for me to vindicate my own rights and let the bond of peace and love be affected or for me to renounce my rights and permit the bond of peace and love to remain between me and the people involved in the situation?

The fact we love God compels us to prefer peace in the situation rather than fighting for our own rights, which is a manifestation of love for others. In renouncing our rights, we show them we consider them, and we love them as ourselves.

This being said, we always have to consider what is best for the people involved in the challenging situation. Sometimes, The Holy Spirit may show us not to give the people what they want, because it is better for them.

This is why love always flows with the Holy Spirit anyway. The Father God, Jesus and the Holy Spirit are one; so if God is Love, then the Holy Spirit is Love, and leads us in how to manifest Him.

We have to be led by the Holy Spirit in everything and every situation, because He is perfect Love and knows all things and discerns all depths. The main decision to make consists in whether to let Him rule over us to love or to let our ego predominate.

2- See the best in people

A second key that can help us manifest God's love is to see the positive in people. There are people who are not easily lovable to us, but we can always find something beautiful and positive in them, for there is a treasure of God in each of His creatures. Focusing on the beauty of God in them helps us honor them and treat them with respect.

People around us also represent a gift to us, even the things in them that are difficult for us to understand or get along with. As all things work together for our good, the things in people that bother us are actually a tool in God's hands to perfect us. The people around us, and even the ones we don't naturally love or the ones who make our lives harder, actually serve for our good. It can also be interesting to keep in mind to learn to see everyone as a gift, a blessing, which can help us love them. We have to learn to celebrate all things as permitted in our lives to make us grow.

We can also try to understand the motives and intentions of people we don't get along with easily, rather than immediately judging their behavior. Empathy helps us see the situation differently than only through our own point of view, and it enables grace.

3- See others like superiors as yourself

Humility is one of the criteria of love mentioned in 1 Corinthians 13. To consider others as being superior to ourselves is not natural or easy to do. The natural tendency of most people is exactly the opposite: we think through our own experience that we know better. Our experience, or what we have learned, gives us confidence in our own judgement. But if we consider the experience of others, it can enrich our perception or understanding of things. The Bible says that men have received gifts from God. Some of these gifts are natural and some are spiritual. In the body of Christ, we have this understanding of being complementary to one another. It's important to have this comprehension of who we are in Christ and who we are to each other; we need each other as we corporately form His body. We are interdependent. This is why the Bible recommends us to consider one another as being superior to ourselves.

This principle leads us to love others. It enables respect, honor, and love.

4- Do to others what you would like them to do to you

Doing to others what we would like them to do to us is a biblical principle that is a practical way of loving. To practice this is a demonstration of loving others like we love ourselves in a practical way. This includes all kinds of works, services, and righteousness, but also attitudes that show respect and honor. In doing that, we show others that we consider them. It also implies that we consider their interest better than our own.

One essential thing we can do for others is prayer. We all need prayer, and the Bible exhorts us to pray for all men. To pray for the people God puts around us is the first mission He gives us. We cannot pray all the time for everybody, but

The Holy Spirit will always show us the people He needs us to pray for. Prayer is more than effective, and it contributes to the blessing of the people we pray for. Prayer is also a manifestation of our love for people.

5- Love surpasses all law

Jesus showed us how to love during His ministry on earth. When He healed the sick during the Sabbath, as the Pharisees were rebuking Him for transgressing the law, He healed them anyway because He was compelled by compassion. He wanted the sick to recover, no matter what the circumstances were. He also sometimes took the risk to be revealed to the people as the Son of God before the pre-determined time of His resurrection. For Him to be revealed as the Son of God to the people before the right time could have caused the divine plan of His Salvation through the cross to fail. It could have pushed the doctors of the law to make Him die earlier and not in the way it was meant, at the cross. Several times in the temple, in the synagogues and in the cities, they were pushing and pressing Him in order to kill Him. This is also why He commanded to demons several times not to declare who He was, and He commanded to several who were healed not to make public what He did.

As He and His disciples were walking through the fields during a Sabbath, He let them glean some wheat stalks because they were hungry, even if it was contrary to the law.

Love is at the same time the main key and the main way in God's Kingdom. It surpasses all legalism. Therefore, as God commanded, in all situations love is supposed to be our motivation that compels us, and not legalism. Our actions and works are supposed to come from our love and compassion for others, and not from legalism or any other factor, like fear, vanity, glory, pride, etc.

6- Graciousness

1 Peter 4:8 *"And above all things, have fervent love for one another, for love will cover a multitude of sins."*

Where there is love, there is grace. But where there is grace, grace makes room for love. Our patience, good attitude, and graciousness will always open doors for love. Graciousness is always a factor that favors love. This is the opposite of legalism, condemnation, accusation, reproach, and a contesting attitude, which all create more anger and division.

Grace and graciousness doesn't mean we have to agree with anything and let people treat us however they want. We sometimes have to clearly disagree, and tell the truth, in love. But, as much as possible, we have to operate in grace, peace, and graciousness, knowing that the ultimate purpose for us with each person we enter into contact with is to help them get closer to Jesus and to His whole Word. We are disciple makers with everyone we meet: Christians or non-Christians, and our main tools are our lives, hearts, and attitude.

Graciousness and grace and love are a true reflection of who The Father is.

7- Be real

"Love rejoices with the truth." **Romans 12:9** " *Let love be without hypocrisy.*"

The reason why the Word of God exhorts us to be real with one another is because our carnal nature tends to contain things to protect itself. People in general and many Christians as well operate with mechanisms of defense that prevent them from walking completely in truth with others. They try to protect themselves by hiding at least a part of the truth.

It wasn't how we initially were created though. Remember in the beginning, in Eden, Adam and Eve were nude and innocent. They had no conscience of being nude because of their innocence. This nudity actually represented purity and innocence itself – the fact they had nothing to hide to God, because they were not yet infected by sin. They were a son and daughter in a pure and dependent relationship with God. This is what we are called to be: His sons and daughters. We are His children. Children are real. The Bible exhorts us to be real with our God, as He is our Father and knows what we need and what we are made of. We are invited to come with confidence before the Throne of His grace, because of Jesus's redemption through which we have access to the same initial position we were made for from eternity: being His children.

If God wants us to be real with Him, which is a demonstration of our love for Him and of the degree of communion we want with Him, He also wants us to be real with others. Most Christians fail to be entirely real with others though. It shouldn't be so. Those mechanisms of defense we engage in mostly come from fear. Fear of judgment, of rejection, of suffering, insecurity, etc.

How can we get rid of fear?

I will just give the main points on how to have victory against fear, as it is not our main subject here. First of all, there are several kinds of fears: insecurity, panic, fear, anxiety, etc. There is also the kinds of fear involved in a situation where people are not able to be completely real with others, like insecurity, fear of judgment, fear of rejection, fear of suffering, etc.

Jesus has triumphed over all fear. He has won the victory over all powers of darkness. Fear has really been defeated at the Cross. This is the reality, and the key when seeking to overcome fear is (just as for any other power of darkness, sin or sickness) to really realize Jesus has already triumphed over it at the Cross, and believe then that we are already in the benefit of His victory. When we confess, with faith, that we receive the benefit of what Jesus did at the Cross, then we get victory; we make it effective in our lives. This is faith.

To focus on what Jesus did at the Cross is really the key to overcome any power of darkness. He has accomplished all.

Another key in overcoming fear is to seek love. In 1 John 4:18, it is said: "There is no fear in love, but perfect love casts out fear, because fear involves torment. But he who fears has not been made perfect in love." Fear is bounded with egocentrism; it makes people keep things for themselves. But if we pursue love above all, then fear tends to disappear because we first seek to love, serve and bless others, and then seek to protect ourselves.

Being real will always lead to true communication, and true communication leads to love. The Bible says that the Truth sets us free. To be real with others puts us in a position of freedom that allows us to love others more easily. And people will generally appreciate honesty and truth. It's an open door for love.

Love, source of other ways

Love is the main way in God's Kingdom. In seeking His Kingdom first, we have to pursue love above all, as His Kingdom consists in love. This is from love that proceeds all the other ways in His realm. Like the sources that flow from the top of the mountains and feeds rivers, love is the source of any other way in God's reality.

1 Corinthians 13:1-3 "*Though I speak with the tongues of men and angels, but have not love, I have become like sounding brass or a clanging cymbal. And though I have the gift of prophecy, and understand all mysteries and all knowledge, and though I have all faith, so that I could* *remove mountains, but have not love, it profits me nothing."*

Justice, righteousness and works without love are pure legalism. They are dead works. But justice, righteousness and works by love are true righteousness that produces life. The expression of gifts, service, and ministry without love are vain and ineffective. But ministry by love is God's true power; it produces life.

Anything done that is not compelled by love is vain. Love is the very motivation of everything in God's Kingdom, because God is Love, and He does everything by and because of His Love. That is why, in anything that we do, we first need to pursue Love. God is Love; therefore, in pursuing Love, we are pursuing God, who He is, and His ways.

Application, Interactions and priorities

Love doesn't necessarily means to allow anything, in the name of love. Love is not laxism. As God is Love, we have the best example of what love is. In meditating on God's ways and his nature through the Bible, we have a lot to learn about what Love really is. God is justice, righteousness, goodness, Holiness, Truth, Light, wisdom, Knowledge, and power combined. He gives us more than we could think or imagine; this means that He doesn't always answer our prayers or our desires the way we would have expected. He wants the best for us, which also means a higher price for us to pay sometimes. His love includes correction, rebuking. It allows suffering in our lives for our growth, for the work of patience and maturity in us. The sum of all this is that His love seeks the best for us, which is not always what we want.

His love for us is a passionate but also a balanced love that seeks our best. Along with God's love for us, our love for others needs to seek the best for them. The only thing we know about what is best for people is for them to know Jesus, to walk according to His plans and purposes for them, being incorporated in the body of Christ, to live by and according to His Word, to live His peace and joy by the Holy Spirit. Therefore, our purpose as disciples and friends of God needs be doing what is possible for them to walk in all this. We are meant to be bridges between people and God. We are meant to lay down our lives to help people live all that God has for them, whether they are Christians or not. We should be able to see every person we meet as God sees them, and we are supposed to do what God puts before us to allow them to live all of this. So everything in our attitudes, actions, and words needs to be led by the vision of this ultimate purpose of love that God has for them. It very often implies that we renounce our own interests, desires or rights, but it also can mean correcting them in love according to the scriptures, or refusing them what they want, if needed.

We need to do everything possible to create or keep the bond of peace as much as it depends on us, and to respond in the challenging situations with the wisdom that comes from the meditation of the whole scripture, and not just some isolated verses.

If we are led by true love, we know we are led by Him. **1 John 4:12** "*If we love one another, God abides in us, and His love has been perfected in us* ." And if we are led by Him, He leads us into His love.

Activation

1-Think of a current or recent situation where you are or were challenged to love and you don't or didn't know what to do.

2-Take a moment with God and ask Him to see the situation with His eyes.

3-Identify the obstacles to love in the situation: in the people involved and inside of yourself (pride, fear, judgement, offense, disagreement, misunderstanding, disappointment, rejection, difference, anger, unforgiveness, etc.).

4-Take a position against these obstacles, in blessing the people involved with the opposite (such as: peace, healing, restoration, adoption, comfort, understanding of their identity in Christ, etc.). If some obstacles come from within you, renounce them. If necessary, forgive. If necessary, repent and receive what God wants to give you instead of what you renounced.

5-Ask God to show you your part in how to keep the bond of peace.

6-Ask God to show you what you can concretely do to restore unity and love toward the people involved in the situation.

7-If there are several things that are shown to you, prioritize them and do them step by step.

The answer from God is always conformed to His word. The sum of His word is the truth, and not only one isolated verse. It's important to be aware that you not make any decision based on one verse only, but to consider that the whole Bible teaches us about God's heart and ways.

2 WAY OF HOLINESS

Holiness is fundamental in the kingdom of God. Because God is holy, all that He does is holy, and all our ways are supposed to be holy. We are called to walk in holiness. The Bible says that without holiness, no one can see The Lord. Holiness is one of the most important witnesses that we belong to God. This is a distinctive mark that we are God's people.

Holiness is the nature of God. If we want to walk according to God, there is no other possibility but to walk in holiness. It is a main way in God's kingdom.

God is Holy

God is Holy. Holiness is one of the most important qualities of God.

Isaiah 6:3 *"Holy, Holy, Holy is the Lord of hosts, the whole earth is full of His glory."*

The Hebraic root of the word "holiness", or "holy", has two fundamental meanings. It can mean:

1. "set apart for an exclusive role", "separated"

2. "brightness", in correlation with absolute purity, the Glory of God

The Hebraic word "kadosh" means pure at all levels: physically, morally, spiritually.

The New Testament uses the term "hagios" which also means "separated, consecrated, set apart" (Luke 2:22), but it most often means "pure". To be holy means not having a spot or wrinkle, or any such thing (Ephesians 5:27). To be holy is an absolute brightness that is not spoiled by anything, a perfect light without any shadow or dark point. The notion of being separated means being separated from sin, being in a perfect state of purity, in the biblical thought.

God is perfectly pure, Holy, and full of majesty. In holiness, there are at the same time the notions of light, truth, righteousness and purity. Holiness inspires respect and godly fear because it represents a power in itself. The angels in heavens continually proclam the holiness of God, crying "Holy, Holy, Holy is the Lord of hosts." God is Light, Truth, Righteousness and purity all together. There is no shadow in Him. The demons flee before His holiness. This is why we can get more victories in fasting and prayer; when we fast, we set ourselves apart to spend some time with the living and Holy God, and His holiness impacts our subjects of prayer and the people we pray for. The room that is normally filled with food and earthly pleasures is then filled with His presence and Holiness, and the demons cannot resist that, so they flee. Holiness is a power.

We are sanctified

Holiness is not a feeling. It's not what we think we are or we are not, but it's a way we can walk in, following Jesus, seeking God. The more we spend some time with The Holy God, the more we become like Him. Seeking Him with a genuine heart and spending some quality time with Him allows us to know Him better, and knowing Him makes us love Him more, which makes us want to please Him.

Even before being a way we can walk in, holiness is a legal status in Christ Jesus.

1 Corinthians 1:30 *"But of Him you are in Christ Jesus, who became for us wisdom from God, and righteousness and sanctification and redemption."*

Our faith in Jesus as the Son of God who came to redeem, save, and reconcile humanity with God the Father automatically gives us a legal status of sanctified and justified people before God, by Jesus's sacrifice at the Cross. At the Cross, Jesus paid the price of our justification and sanctification. He has cancelled our sins and made us clean before God. God sees us as clean, pure and sanctified before the blood of Jesus. This is a "legal" spiritual status that cannot change unless we decide to deliberately walk in sin and walk away from God.

As Christians, we are sanctified. This is the free gift of His grace. Nevertheless, the Bible exhorts us to *"walk worthy of the calling with which"* we were called (**Ephesians 4:1**). We live under an amazing status of grace that grants us sanctification as given in advance, but it is our part to persevere in it.

Sanctification is given to us as an inheritance, and it is our part to continually walk in it. As children of God, we can make mistakes, and we can sometimes fail to do what is right. We can easily sin if we are not continually connected with the one who never sinned. But we are assured that all our sins are forgiven if we repent. Past, present and future sins are cancelled if we don't intentionally and consistently commit them to provoke God, and if we truly repent. **Hebrews 10:26** "*For if we sin willfully after we have received the knowledge of the truth, there no longer remains a sacrifice for sins, but a certain fearful expectation of judgment and fiery indignation which will devour the adversaries.*"

Jesus is our sanctification, given as an inheritance. All is done. We are sanctified already. Nothing of what we can do or not do will change this status, because Jesus has paid for it with His own life. The price for it has been too high for God to change His mind about it. It is done. Nevertheless, like for any inheritance, we have to steward it. Jesus is our sanctification, and if we want to walk in this amazing inheritance, we need to pursue Jesus. We are supposed to pursue holiness.

Hebrews 12:14 "*Pursue peace with all people, and holiness without which no one will see The Lord.*"

Called to walk in holiness

1 Peter 1:15-16 "*But as He who called you is Holy, you also* *be holy in all your conduct; because it is written 'be holy, for I am holy.'"* Holiness is a distinctive mark of the people of God. We are called to be holy as He is holy. Holiness is a testimony of who God is: the opposite of sin.

This verse mentions our conduct; it shows that holiness is a way we can walk in. We can be holy in all our conduct. We can walk in holiness in everything that we think, do or say. Holiness is the opposite of sin, darkness, and unrighteousness. Therefore we are called to walk in light, truth, purity, and righteousness in all our conduct. The command "be holy, for I am holy" not only exhorts us to imitate God in His nature, but is a declaration of God Himself upon us that we are able to be holy because of His holiness.

If we have received sanctification as an inheritance from God, through Jesus's sacrifice, we need to be willing to walk in this inheritance. As with many things we receive by grace, we are requested to steward the things that are given to us by an act of decision. We have to decide to walk in holiness continually, and collaborate with God for that to be able to enjoy our inheritance. In each situation, we have to decide which way to take: holiness or flesh. But the more we grow in the communion with the One who is Holy, the more we become like Him.

How can we walk in holiness?

The only way of walking in holiness is to seek God and to let Him soak His nature in us.

If we want to walk in holiness, we need to spend some time with the God of holiness. We need to come to Him in worship and let Him minister to us with His love, with his consolation and restoration. This is the best way to be transformed to His image, from glory to glory. Worshiping in truth and spirit makes us focus on His glory, and not on our issues, which allows His grace to operate in us. True worship can powerfully transform us because we are focused on what Jesus did at the Cross, and the proclamation of His triumph over death and darkness. When we proclaim with faith the reality of the Cross, then it becomes a reality in our lives. "The righteous will live by faith." True proclamation and worship are a demonstration of faith, and it is by faith that we receive the promises of salvation, healing, adoption, and all blessings.

The simple act of spending some time with God, in a true relationship, seeking His presence, makes our communion with Him grow, makes us love Him more, and makes us want to become like Him. It makes His holiness soak in us and grow in us.

It is only through the communion with His Spirit, who is holy, that we can walk in holiness. To have a more precise idea of what holiness is and what it looks like to walk in holiness, the best way is to examine the fruits of the Spirit, who is the Holy Spirit of God. The fruits of the Spirit reveal the characteristics of the Spirit of God who is Holy. They are a declaration of what holiness is.

The fruit of the Spirit

Galatians 5:16-23 "*I say then: walk in the Spirit and you shall not fulfill the lust of the flesh. For the flesh lusts against the Spirit, and the Spirit against the flesh; and these are contrary to one another, so that you do not do the things that you wish. But if you are led by the Spirit, you are not under the law. Now, the works of the flesh are evident, which are: adultery, fornication, uncleanness, lewdness, idolatry, sorcery, hatred, contentions, jealousies, outbursts of wrath, selfish ambitions, dissentions, heresies, envy, murders, drunkenness, revelries, and the like ; of which I tell you beforehand, just as I also told you in time past, that those who practice such things will not inherit the kingdom of God.*"

But the fruit of the Spirit is love, joy, peace, longsuffering, kindness, goodness, faithfulness, gentleness, self-control. *Against such there is no law. And those who are Christ's have crucified the flesh with its passions and desires. If we live in the Spirit, let us also walk in the Spirit. Let us not become conceited, provoking one another, envying one another."*

To walk in holiness we need to walk in the Spirit. To walk in the Spirit means to walk according to, and with, the Spirit of God, and not according to the flesh. It is a choice, and a way of life. Walking in the flesh is the opposite of walking in holiness, because the flesh only produces sin. The examples of sin produced by the flesh are mentioned in this verse. In examining the list of those sins as the opposite of what we are supposed to live in holiness, we can have an idea of what represents holiness according to God's heart. The opposite of adultery, fornication, uncleanness and lewdness are purity and faithfulness. The opposite of idolatry, sorcery, revelries and heresies are to love God and adore Him only as well as faithfulness, purity, and contentment. The opposite of selfish ambition, hatred, contentions, jealousies, and envy are love and goodness. The opposite of wrath, dissentions, murders, and drunkenness are peace and self-control.

We can therefore identify as characteristics of holiness:

-to love God and adore Him only

-love

-purity

-peace

-faithfulness

-contentment-joy

-goodness, kindness, gentleness

-self-control

Those characteristics are actually the same as the ones mentioned as fruits of the Spirit. There are three other characteristics in the list of the fruits of the Spirit: gentleness, kindness, and longsuffering, which complete the characteristics found in analyzing the opposite of the works of the flesh.

To adore and serve God only is actually the first command: "*You shall love and serve your God only.*" It is actually a gift that comes from Himself, to adore Him and serve Him. This gift grows with the communion with Him, and in faithfulness. It is then normal we don't find it as a fruit of the Spirit, because it comes before we get to walk in the Spirit. Nevertheless, we can consider that once we start to walk in the Spirit, it contributes to keeping our communion with God alive.

To adore God and serve Him only

To love God is the first characteristic of holiness. It is the first command of God. God is holy, and when we love Him, we love His holiness. When we come to Him with a sincere heart to follow Him, we embrace His holiness. We cannot live in holiness unless we are in communion with the only true God, who is Holy. Outside of a relationship with God, there is no holiness. Outside of a communion with the true God, people can live law, religion, legalism, and self-righteousness, but no holiness. Holiness can only be found in a true communion with God.

Also, allegiance to the only one true God is the key for holiness. If we approach God but still practice idolatry, then it means that we don't let God rule completely over our lives, and we block the access of His holiness in us. Idolatry is anything that we put before God, to adore. Anything that can take the place of God in our lives. It can be other gods (which are demons), ourselves (egocentrism: when we love ourselves more than God and make our decisions according to what pleases us, and not to what pleases Him. The fact of being focused on what we want, what we are, what we need, rather than Who He is, what He wants), people: members of family (children, parents, husband, wife, etc.) that we love more than God, etc. Idolatry is a sin and opposite to holiness, as it is unfaithfulness toward God.

As children of God, we are not supposed to let anything take the place of God in our lives. God is God whether we follow Him or not. When we love something or someone more than God in our lives, we actually reject God as God. We make Him inferior or smaller than who He really is; we deteriorate the communion with Him, and we block the access of His blessings for us.

God is able to respond to any need in us. He is more than sufficient to fill any need or desire in us. He is our Father, the one who provides for us, the One who knows better than us what is best for us.

Nobody can love us like Our Heavenly Father loves us. He demonstrated His love in giving His precious Son to die instead of us. He watches over us, takes care of us, protects us, and walk before us, He makes us take part in His Glory and His eternal plan for Humanity, and He shares everything with us. He is the author of our lives, and with each of our lives, He has a plan and purpose for us to live on Earth with Him. Therefore, He only is worthy to be adored and exalted in our lives. He only is worthy to be the number one in our lives, to hold the first place in our hearts.

In adoring God only, we allow Him to be King in our lives; we entirely accept His sovereignty upon us, and we let His holiness be established in us. When we give our lives to God, we invite Him to live in us with all of who He is, including His holiness, and to reign in us. We actually renounce our own lives to live in complete surrendering to Him. This is all that we are supposed to live as His people. Holiness then looks like being one with Him.

Love

A second major characteristic of holiness is love. A major part of walking in holiness is walking in love. We know that God is love, and we don't walk in holiness if we don't walk in love.

The works of the flesh described in Galatians 5 are opposed to love: hatred, adultery, contentions, jealousies, outbursts of wrath, selfish ambitions, dissentions, envy, and murders. This list gives us by opposition an idea of what it looks like to pursue love without succumbing to the flesh and its traps. To seek what is best for others, and not be led by our own interests or desires. It shows us how we have to take a position against the powers of darkness that will try to tempt us to depart from the way of love. If those things or such are in our lives, we have to renounce them, by a simple act of decision, invoking the Cross that set us free from any darkness. We have to decide to pursue love instead, and let God help us reeducate us to live in love, in those areas that were inhabited by darkness.

For each of those areas, we can have the victory because Jesus already had the victory over them. We can identify the things in our lives that are opposite to love and adopt a strategy to overcome them. Let's take the example of hatred. Hatred is easy to identify because it is in general what we can feel for a person we really dislike. Hatred is sin. It is the complete opposite of love. If we notice we feel hatred toward somebody, the problem doesn't come from the other person, but the problem is the sin of hatred itself in us. We have to deal with it. Moreover, someone who has hatred in them generally does not feel hatred only for one person, but for several people, depending on if the sin has had time or room to grow in them.

1 John 4:20-21 *"If someone says 'I love God' and hates his* *brother, he is a liar; for he who does not love his brother whom he has seen, how can he love God whom he has not seen? And this commandment we have from Him: that he who loves God must love His brother also."*

To overcome hatred, we first have to confess it to God and repent. We have to realize that it is not ours, but a trap from the enemy to prevent us from walking in freedom to love. Once we realize it, we renounce it. When we renounce it, we confirm we want it to be replaced by God's love. This is the first step. The second step is to pray for the people we have hatred for. We bless them, and we ask God for His love for these people. We can pray for God to show us things that can help us love these people, or to help us see them as He sees them. We can declare what they are to us (colleagues, brother or sister in Christ, family member, etc.) and thank God for them in our lives. Then comes the third step, which consists of reeducating (or training) ourselves to love, each time hatred tries to come back. This is a training that demands effort, but it works. This battle first takes place in our mind. When a thought of hatred comes in our mind, we need to immediately replace it with a thought of love and blessing. This is a training that can take a while, but it absolutely works if we persevere. This training works for any other darkness we need to get rid of to walk in God's Light.

Once we start winning the battle of thoughts, then attitudes become easy to change as well, with the same principle.

Pursuing love involves identifying what in our lives fights against love, renouncing those things, and reeducating ourselves to walk in God's Light and love.

God has two most important desires for us to live, not for Himself but for our good. The first one is for us to love Him and be one with Him. The second one is to love others like ourselves. These two main desires of His heart are actually the two first commandments, and they resume the whole law. They both represent an important part of what holiness is. In truly loving others, we show that we love God and that we take part in His Holiness.

Purity

We have seen that holiness means purity. We are called to holiness; therefore, we are called to purity. Purity exists at several different levels: spiritual purity, purity of heart, and physical purity. These three levels of purity are bound together and they interact with one another.

Spiritual purity

The first level of purity touches our spirit and our spiritual activity. Spiritual purity is being one with the true living God, and Him only. A lot of things can deteriorate this oneness and communion: idolatry, sorcery, occultism, religion, etc. These are spiritual impurities. God considers these as spiritual adultery. We see how many times in the Old Testament God mentions "adultery", the fact His people was serving other gods. The Bible says that we cannot be in communion with Him if we have communion with the demons. Any god other than the true living God is a demon. They are spiritual principalities of darkness. Any spiritual activity that is outside the communion with the true living God is impure. It is sin. God considers the relationship with His people as a covenant; this is why He called the unfaithfulness of His people adultery, when they turned their hearts to other gods. This is still occurring today: if we are His people, we take part in a covenant with Him. This covenant is the New Covenant through Jesus Christ. We were made to be one with our creator, the author of our lives and of the whole universe. We were made to be His children and have communion with Him. We are called to a wonderful relationship with our Heavenly Father. This is the only pure spiritual activity.

Purity of heart

Purity of heart is the second level of purity. It corresponds to the whole area of mind, thoughts, and heart. **Proverbs 23:7** *"For as he thinks in his heart, so is he."*

Philippians 4:8 *"Finally, Brethren, whatever things are true, whatever things are noble, whatever things are just, whatever things are pure, whatever things are lovely, whatever things are of good report, if there is any virtue, and if there is anything praiseworthy; meditate on these things."*

This whole area can be resumed as the activity of the soul. The heart and the soul can be filled with whatever we let them be filled with. They are like a sponge that absorbs what we feed them. There are three sources that can feed our thoughts: The Spirit of God, our own heart, and the devil. We can identify the source of our thoughts and we have the authority to steward them. Our thoughts are filled with what we let them be filled with. The more we nourish our soul with the Word of God, the more our thoughts are Christ-like and *"into captivity to the obedience of Christ."* The more we nourish our soul with our own heart, the more our thoughts will be carnal. And if we accept thoughts that are not conformed to the thought of God, we give the enemy access to our thoughts.

Our soul is like a field where the major battle of our lives takes place. Several armies are enlisted in this battle: the thoughts of God, the thoughts of the flesh-heart, and the thoughts of the enemy. The thoughts of God are meant to edify us, encourage us, remind us who we are in Christ, and guide us. They are meant to lead us to victory if we sympathize with them and exercise them. Their outcome is life. The thoughts of the enemy are meant to discourage us, to lie to us, to lead us to sin, depression and defeat. Their outcome is death. Depending on how we nourish our soul, the thoughts of our own heart can be either tinged with the thoughts of God or the thoughts of the enemy. The more we nourish our soul with God's thoughts, the more our heart becomes like His heart. But if we don't, then it is an easy ground for the enemy to occupy. Therefore, the thoughts of our heart can either be an ally to the army of God's thoughts or to the army of the enemy's thoughts.

Spiritual purity is essential to win the battle of the thoughts and to make our heart pure. If our spirit is in communion with the Spirit of God, and if we practice His thoughts, we make our heart His holy field. We see then the interaction between spiritual purity and purity of heart. We can only be pure through the communion with God.

Physical purity

Physical purity is the third level of purity. It is directly linked to the two other levels. If our spirit is pure, then our heart can be pure. If our heart is pure, then our physical conduct will be pure. Our body is the temple of the Holy Spirit. God lives in us, and it is our responsibility to keep our body pure. **Romans 12:1** "*I beseech you therefore, brethren, by the mercies of God, that you present your bodies a living sacrifice, holy, acceptable to God, which is your reasonable service. And do not be conformed to this world, but be transformed by the renewing of your mind, that you may prove what is that good and acceptable and perfect will of God.*"

Hebrews 13:4 "*Marriage is honorable among all, and the bed undefiled; but fornicators and adulterers God will judge.*"

In many Scriptures, the Word of God warns us against physical impurity. Physical impurity often reveals an impure spirit. Spiritual impurity is often an open door to physical impurity. Like when Israel made the golden calf, they immediately fell into debauchery. This is why the main key to overcoming impurity is to seek oneness and communion with God as a priority.

We are called to keep our body a holy temple for God. We

won't enumerate here the multiple ways of living in impurity, because the enemy knows how to do his own advertisement. But we would rather like to present the beauty of living in pure conduct. As we are the temple of the Holy Spirit, we know in our spirit what honors Him and what does not honor Him, like in marriage we know what honors the spouse or not. God has planned everything for us to live a live of contentment at any level. If we walk by His Spirit in every area, we have access to the greatest contentment He has planned for us to live. Physical satisfaction is reserved for marriage, and the greatest physical satisfaction is reserved in marriage for the pure hearted spouse (Hebrews 13:4).

If we love God, we know what pleases Him, and our physical conduct reflects our hearts toward Him. Physical purity is a major aspect of holiness.

It is our responsibility to steward any of these three levels of activity. We make our own choices and we are responsible for our decisions, as we were given free will.

Peace

Peace is a way of God in itself and is a part of holiness. If we want to walk in holiness, we need to pursue peace as well. Peace is both the fruit of decision and a fruit of the Spirit. The examples of the opposite of peace mentioned in Galatians 5 are "contentions", "dissentions" and "wrath". They are all the works of the flesh. Both "contentions" and "dissentions" are actions that we decide, whereas "wrath" is more the manifestation of a character.

Contentions and dissentions are a manifestation of opposition and disagreement, but not in a peaceful way. It is easy to walk in peace when we agree on everything with everybody. But the challenge comes with disagreement. Peace is the ability of dealing with disagreement in a way that doesn't break unity. This can be operated in several ways, according to the situation and the stakes.

The first thing we need to do in a situation of disagreement is to evaluate what is right according to God's word and God's thought in the situation. This can immediately position us as to what we have to stand for. Several scenarios can occur.

1- If we realize we need to realign our position to what is right according to God's word, then it is easy to reposition ourselves and come in agreement with the other person.

2- If our position is conformed to God's word and thought and the other part is obviously not, then the truth must be exposed in peace, and we can try to lead the other person to review their own position. Two possibilities can result from this: the person agrees to reposition herself according to God's word and thought or the person doesn't want to reposition herself. In that case, we have to do our part to stand in conformity with the Word of God and with what is right, as much as it depends on us, and in an attitude that doesn't reject the person herself. It is important when we disagree with a person because of her unrighteousness (or non-conformity to the Word of God) to stand for what is biblically right, but to show the person we don't reject her but the unrighteousness. In this situation this is the only way to manifest peace.

3- If both positions are conformed to the Word of God, then we have to evaluate if our position is worthy enough to risk the bond of peace to be broken. The question is: what is the most worthy in the situation, my position to be held or the bond of peace to be kept? Then, two different decisions can be taken: either to surrender our position, because we consider it is more important for the bond of peace not to be broken, or to keep our position because we think it is the best, considering the whole situation. In that last case, it is then important to do it in a way that shows respect to the person involved, our motives being clearly expressed in a peaceful way.

The other opposite of peace is "outburst of wrath," anger. It is the manifestation of a sinful character, or sometimes a spirit of anger. In that area, peace as a fruit of the Spirit is to be exercised. We know that the fruit of the Spirit is a result of communion with God and choosing to walk in His Spirit (Galatians 5:16). Jesus is the Prince of Peace. Peace is one of the main characteristics of God. The more time we spend with the Prince of Peace, the more peace is established in our hearts.

Faithfulness

Revelations 19:11 "*Now I saw heaven opened, and behold, a white horse. And He who sat on him was called Faithful and True.*"

It is interesting to see that faithfulness is a part of holiness. God is faithful. He is described many times as faithful in the Bible. It is a part of His nature.

A large number of synonyms can be related to the term of "faithfulness" which give understanding of its meaning: "fidelity", "constant", "loyal", "reliable", "maintaining allegiance", "trustworthiness", "marked by or showing a strong sense of duty or responsibility", "true", "conscientious", etc. According to some definitions founds in dictionaries[1], the adjective "faithful" implies a *"steadfast adherence to a person or thing to which one is bound as by an oath or obligation."* The adjective "loyal", which is close to its meaning, implies an *"undeviating allegiance to a person or cause, etc., which one feels morally bound to support or defend."*

God is faithful by nature, and is faithful to always honor the covenant with His people and the promises to His people. He is faithful by nature and by decision. He is constant in all His ways.

Faithfulness is a characteristic of holiness, which is interesting to meditate on when we notice that it is a rare quality to find. Only a few people manifest faithfulness in all areas. Some may be only faithful in certain areas, those they probably consider the most important for them, but most people are not faithful in all areas of life. Yet, faithfulness is a fruit of the Spirit, which if we walk in it is supposed to make us faithful in all things, as God is faithful in all things. The Bible says that if we are not faithful in small things, then we are not faithful in greater things. God considers faithfulness as a reflection of His character. We are supposed to walk in it. And because He is faithful, we

---

1   Le Larousse French Dictionary, Le Petit Robert French Dictionary

are able to be faithful by His Spirit in all things.

One main reason why faithfulness is important and precious to God's eyes is that it is a component of love. Faithfulness doesn't disappoint. Faithfulness honors the people we interact with. It doesn't allow people to be disappointed. It allows the bound of love to be maintained.

First of all, God expects us to be faithful to Him. As we know, we are supposed to be one with Him, in a communion of love. In the Bible, the relationship between God and His people is often described as a marriage. It is often spoken about Jesus and the Church, like the Husband and His Bride; and the prophets of the Old Testament often used the vocabulary of marriage to describe the relationship between God and His people. Marriage actually is a reflection of the relationship between Jesus and The Church. It is a holy communion that is supposed to reflect the communion between God and His people. This is why God loves marriage so much. Like in marriage, faithfulness is expected at all levels in our relationship with God; communion with Him only, adoration of Him only, works, services, tithes and offerings, etc. In marriage, faithfulness doesn't only consist in not falling into adultery, but it consists also in a faithfulness of heart that doesn't covet others. It consists also in encouraging, helping, supporting, etc. It is a

76

commitment at all levels, just as with our relationship with God.

Secondly, God expects us to be faithful in general in our commitment to others: family, church, work, relationships, friendships, etc. God loves faithfulness because by our faithfulness, we demonstrate our love.

1 Timothy 5:8 *"But if anyone does not provide for his own, and especially for those of his household, he has denied the faith, and is worse than an unbeliever."*

Faithfulness is truly a mark of a godly character. The world in which we live encourages unfaithfulness in every area. But it is our responsibility to *"not be conformed to this world, but be transformed by the renewing of -our- minds, that -we- may prove what is that good and acceptable and perfect will of God."* (**Romans 12:2**).

Also, faithfulness is a witness that can impact the life of people around us. It is a component of love and holiness that can draw people to God.

Contentment- joy

Philippians 4:4 *"Rejoice in the Lord always. Again I will say, rejoice!"*

One of the fruits of the Spirit is joy. As a fruit of the Spirit, it is therefore included in what holiness is. The Holy Spirit is joyful. We are able to walk in joy, whatever the circumstances are, because of the Holy Spirit in us.

Joy according to the world is temporary and short, variable depending on the circumstances. It is a superficial emotion that fluctuates depending on if one gets what one desires or covets, and it often immediately ends once one gets it. It cannot be compared to the true joy that only God can give us. In **2 Corinthians 6:10**, Paul mentions the fact that, as Christians, we can be *"sorrowful, yet always rejoicing."* As Christians, even when we are in a midst of circumstances that can legitimately bring us sorrow, we have an inner joy that remains. This permanent joy is bound to our identity in Jesus Christ and to our hope: children of God, reconciled with the Father, coheirs with Christ, seated with Him in the Holy places.

Godly joy is not a superficial feeling or emotion, but it is a deep contentment that takes root in who we are in Jesus. Therefore, circumstances are not supposed to take away our joy. We can remain in that joy as long as we remain in communion with the Holy Spirit. Godly contentment has nothing to do with pasting a fake smile on one's face; it is a true inner happiness that comes from our communion with

God. It is a gift and a fruit of our communion with God, and not something superficial we pretend to have. Because it is known that as Christians we are supposed to remain in joy, some Christians can be seen forcing themselves to seem happy or joyful while they are not. This is a carnal reaction to protect oneself of judgment, while not living the fruit of the Spirit.

The trap of the enemy is to try to steal our joy through bad circumstances. Our force is to keep our eyes on the author of our joy and see all circumstances as good for us, as we know that "*all things work together for our good.*" Joy and contentment is a characteristic of holiness first because God is joyful, and because it is rooted in the hope of eternal and abundant life with God. To remain in His joy is a part of remaining in communion with Him and walking in His Spirit.

Another way of losing our joy is sin. Sin puts a wall between us and God, which spoils the communion with Him. If the communion with Him is broken, then we cannot live in His joy anymore. This is also why joy is a part of holiness; it is a mark that we live in His will.

Goodness, Kindness, Gentleness

Goodness, kindness and gentleness, as fruits of the Spirit,

are another facet of holiness. They are a part of what love is. They honor others and show them attention and respect. They seek other people's good and interests. Some of their opposites are: egocentrism, egoism, jealousy, envy, wickedness, etc. These are the works of the flesh and sin.

Goodness is a quality that covers other people's faults and that seeks their good. It is a blessing heart that wants the best for others, not only in intentions but also in actions. God is always our example in everything, and God is good. He wants the best for us. He has the best intentions and the best plans for us. He assures us that "*all things work together for our good.*" As goodness is a part of God's love for us, it must be a part of our love for others. If we live by His Spirit, then goodness should automatically characterize us.

Kindness is pretty close to goodness in its meaning. But it is more a character that seeks to accommodate, to please, to serve others. It is another level of goodness. In kindness there is more of a notion of proximity, affection, and tenderness of heart. It is interesting to notice that it is listed in the fruits of the Spirit because it actually reveals a facet of the Holy Spirit. The Spirit of God is more than good with us; He is kind with us. His kindness can soak in us, if we dwell in Him. Then we can be kind as we should be toward others.

Gentleness is close to kindness, with maybe more of the notion of forgetting oneself in being kind to others. It is another level of kindness. Gentleness is a character that loves and seeks to please and serve others no matter what. It is very interesting to note it is a character of the Holy Spirit, as it is listed in His fruits. God is not only good and kind, but He is also gentle with us. His gentleness can become ours toward others, if we seek Him.

Holiness then implies a deep level of love and attention to others. The Bible speaks about having a "*fervent love*" for one another. Goodness, kindness and gentleness are some expressions of that love. If they are mentioned as fruits of the Spirit, they are not an option, but a true standard for us to live. It is only in cherishing the communion with our God, in delighting in the beauty and the depth of His love for us, that we can receive this ability to walk in true goodness, kindness and gentleness.

Self-Control

There is nothing surprising in the fact that self-control is a condition for holiness. Self-control is the ability to rule over one's flesh. Our spirit is the part of our being that commands most of our actions. The activity of our spirit impacts the activity of our soul (thoughts, minds and heart), and the activity of our soul impacts our actions and attitudes. If our spirit is in communion with God's Spirit, and if we let Him rule over us, then our actions, reactions and attitudes are conformed to His will and His holiness. This is what it means "to walk in the Spirit."

Galatians 5:16-23 "*I say then: walk in the Spirit and you shall not fulfill the lust of the flesh. For the flesh lusts against the Spirit, and the Spirit against the flesh.*"

Self-control is the ability to control the burst of the flesh, by the authorization we give to the Holy Spirit to rule over us. We then are no longer led by the flesh, but by the Spirit. Self-control is a manifestation of holiness because it is the fruit of the Holy Spirit in us. We have seen that all the works of the flesh are sin and lead to death. The fruits of the Spirit are the expression of God's holiness in us, and they lead to abundant life and joy.

As long as we live on earth, we have to continually stay connected to The Holy Spirit of God, if we want to walk according to Him and not let our flesh be in control. This is the key for life. How does it concretely work? The key is truly communion with God – the more we enjoy spending time in His presence, the more we become like Him. There are areas in our lives that are easily transformed into His Glory and some that need more intention, effort, and time. This is the case in particular in the presence of strongholds. Once we get delivered of a stronghold or a devil spirit (this can happen exactly like a healing can happen: instantly through prayer, through a process while intentionally seeking God in fasting and prayer, in a moment of worship, etc.), we often have to reeducate ourselves to live without the stronghold or the spirit. They were occupying a room that now is ready to be filled with what is the opposite in the Spirit of God.

The opposite of self-control is letting anything from the flesh take control. This is disorder. The Bible says that we become slaves of what we let ourselves be subject to. Anger, fear, wrath, passions, lust, impurity, etc. – any sin can be eradicated from our lives, first because Jesus already took them at The Cross. Self-control is first the act of will to steward our thoughts that lead to our actions. Managing our thoughts becomes easier when we fill our soul with the thoughts of God, with His Word. To maintain a connection between our Spirit and His Spirit is a sure way of walking in victory and self-control.

We see that holiness includes a wide range of characteristics that are all complementary to one another. Holiness is actually the opposite of sin. We could mention many more characteristics of holiness, as those mentioned here are only a few of them. Humility, obedience, faith, resting in God, honor, loyalty, patience, longsuffering are some more characteristics of holiness we could have listed here. But the Holy Spirit who teaches us all things is able to show us the things in which we need to align ourselves to walk in His holiness.

Application

First, all the elements that compose holiness are never contradictory or conflicting to one another. They are all complementary and interdependent because holiness is a whole thing. Holiness is actually not only a list of qualities, but it is a way we are meant to walk in. This is a style of life, based on our love for God, whether we walk in holiness or not. We know that there are some areas of our lives that are stronger than others, and that we are in process from Glory to Glory during all our life. But holiness is a matter of heart toward God. If we want to please Him, then we allow Him to do the adjustments that it takes to be conformed to His image. This is why holiness is a way. We walk in it. We are considered sanctified by God, and we are moving from Glory to Glory.

The main key to walk in holiness is to love God, to spend some quality time with Him. It is to remain in a true and sincere communion with Him in which we let Him love on us and minister to us.

Activation

1-Think about the quality of your relationship with God. Are you in a true communion with God?

2-Ask yourself if there is something you can do to restore the communion with Him, or improve the quality of your relationship with Him.

3-Is there any particular area of your life you would like to align with God's character after reading this chapter?

4-If yes, take a moment with God and thank Him for the finished work of Jesus at The Cross. Bring that area to Him (or those, if there are several); renounce it or repent if necessary. And thank Him for the freedom you have in the

Holy Spirit, to walk in newness in that area.

5-You can do that each time you feel God wants you to align some areas of your life with His holiness.

3 WAY OF RIGHTEOUSNESS-GRACE

Psalm 89:14 *"Righteousness and justice are the foundation of your throne; mercy and truth go before your face."*

The third way of God is righteousness and justice. This is a foundation in God's Kingdom. The world today is so full of darkness that people don't know what is right and what is wrong. Even some Christians don't always discern their right and left hand. There is a moral and spiritual blindness that makes people unconscious of what is right and unrighteous. We live in a world where justice for people only means an institution that is supposed to protect their own interest. But righteousness and justice, according to the Bible, is something much greater and higher than this. This is a way of God.

Psalm 11:7 *"For The Lord is righteous, He loves righteousness; His countenance beholds the upright."*

Deuteronomy 32:4 *"He is the Rock, His work is perfect; for all His ways are justice, a God of truth and without injustice; righteous and upright is He."*

God is righteous. He is a God of righteousness and justice. All His ways are righteous. Righteousness is one more attribute of God, and an important way in the Kingdom of God. It is a whole attribute of God in itself, even though we can consider it a combination of love and holiness. The notion of justice, equity, and righteousness is essential throughout the Bible; it is a main component in God's Kingdom. His Kingdom is a kingdom of righteousness and justice. God is spoken of as a judge several times in the Bible.

Like God, we are called to be righteous and to walk in

righteousness. Righteousness, like holiness, cannot be observed like a list of rules and laws, but is a way we can walk in when we understand who God is. Righteousness is more bound to our actions; it is a behavior that is morally and spiritually right. But it is first a character, a mindset that comes from God, to walk in what is right.

In the law of the Old Covenant, in the Old Testament, many rules of conduct are given that reflect the standards of God concerning righteousness. Some of them will be mentioned in this chapter, not as rules to observe, but as significant examples that help in understanding the Spirit of the righteousness of God. We know that as Christians we don't live under the law, but under the Grace of God. We have received, through the faith in Jesus as Son of God, the Holy Spirit of God who lives in us and makes us able to live His standards of righteousness. From this perspective, the main principles of the righteousness of God will be presented in this chapter. The purpose of this chapter is to capture the main principles of God's righteousness, to be able to walk in it or to improve our walk in this way.

What is righteousness?

After the reading of many occurrences of the term

"righteousness" in the Bible, we can define it as a way or a conduct that pleases and honors God and that is conformed to His heart. The word "righteousness" in the Bible generally means following His Word, His ways, to be after His heart, to honor Him and others. It also represents doing what is right, what is good, according to His principles. The meaning of "righteousness" in the Word includes both a righteousness of heart and a conduct that is righteous. It corresponds then both to a character as well as the behavior that comes out it.

Righteousness implies several main qualities, without which there is no righteousness. These qualities will help us to understand that righteousness is a way to walk in, rather than a corpus of rules to follow. This is first a character, a mindset and a disposition of heart that lead us to walk according to the heart of God.

Honesty

Honesty is a main part of righteousness. Without honesty, there cannot be righteousness. Honesty is the character of someone who is dependable, trustworthy, reliable, and honest, who doesn't lie or deceive. Lying and deceitfulness are not reconcilable with righteousness. They are mentioned in the law as things that God absolutely disapproves of. They are the opposite of truth, light and faithfulness included in the notion of honesty. Honesty is both the character and the behavior that manifests what is right. It is the mark of being conscientious before God. In being honest, we manifest that we live under God's light. What God doesn't like about deceitfulness and lying is, more than the sin itself, the fact that he who does such things assumes that God doesn't see it. It shows a lack of faith and consideration toward God. It is first disrespectful toward God who sees everything. Also, what God doesn't like in this sin is that it deceives Him first. God always identifies Himself in what we live; Jesus said that what we do to His people, we do to Him. His spirit lives in us—we have the Holy habitation of God in us—so we are supposed to respect and honor the Spirit of God in others' lives. We see how God is affected by such behavior that doesn't honor Him in others, for example, in the book of Acts, through the story of Ananias and Sapphira. They deceived the assembly of God in pretending to give the totality of the price of their propriety. Peter prophesied that they *"have lied to the Holy Spirit."* (Peter 5:3). We know what happened to them after having done such a thing.

Proverbs 16:11 *"Honest weights and scales are The*

Lord's; all the weights in the bag are His work."

Proverbs 11:1 *"Dishonest scales are an abomination to The Lord, but a just weight is His delight."*

Honesty touches all areas of life. It is first a character that manifests itself in each situation of life: marriage, work, business, finances, etc.

Honesty comes from The Lord. He is Light and Truth, and walking in honesty and righteousness manifests a part of who He is. By His Spirit, we are called to walk in honesty in all areas. Honesty without God does exist, but it is generally partial. An honest character comes from God who created us in His image. When something of His character is manifested in men, it is because we were made like Him. However, it is only by His Spirit that we can manifest a perfect righteousness. His Spirit witnesses all situations of what we are supposed to do and how we are supposed to walk. He is our righteousness.

Justice

The notion of justice is an important part of righteousness. Biblical Justice is making people and society whole, in upholding goodness and impartiality. King David is known for exercising justice during his reign in Israel. He was after

God's heart, saw Israel as God's heritage, and his kingdom was a safe place for the weak, the widows and the orphans.

James 1:27 *"Religion that God our Father accepts as pure and faultless is this: to look after orphans and widows in their distress and to keep oneself from being polluted by the world."*

Proverbs 29:7 *"The righteous care about justice for the poor, but the wicked have no such concern."*

Justice in the Bible takes on at least three aspects: legal, moral and social. When justice is spoken about in the Bible, it generally touches on at least one of these aspects, or all three at the same time. Legal justice represents our justification through Jesus Christ. He was made Justice for us, and we are no longer self-righteous, only through His blood and His grace. This is fundamental to understanding that our justice doesn't come from ourselves or our actions-works, but from the Grace of God who gave Jesus to be our justification. We are considered just by God, simply by our faith in Jesus as the Son of God, our savior and Lord. Also, in receiving Him as Lord, we have received His Holy Spirit that enables us to walk in righteousness and justice. Exactly like holiness, we walk in righteousness and justice because of and with the help of His Spirit in us. Legal justice is then a juridical-spiritual status or situation that approves us as just by the blood of Jesus.

Moral justice is a character and a conduct that manifests God's justice. Through a true communion with God, our character and conduct changes into what pleases God. Our character becomes like His, and we seek what He seeks. The expression of moral justice looks like compassion, goodness, and grace towards others.

Social justice in the Bible consists of setting the captives free from oppression, promoting civil rights, promoting justice in institutions (courts, government, etc.) and the respect of authorities, helping the poor and the weak in society, and integrity in business and family areas.

When the Bible exhorts us to seek first *"The Kingdom of God and Its Justice,"* these three levels are included in the notion of justice. We see that it comes first out of our love for God and communion with Him, that we can seek what pleases Him in every area.

Truth

Jesus said, *"I am the way, the truth and the life."* (John 14:6). God is the Truth. He loves truth and hates everything that is opposite to the truth. Truth is one of the foundations of righteousness. It is not hiding anything that could spoil unity in the Kingdom of God. As children of God we are supposed to live in His light and in His truth. If we love Him, we love truth and light. He is the Truth, and the sum of His Word is truth (Psalm 119:160). If we love Him, we also love His Word that is meant to instruct us and enlighten us on His ways.

We have seen that lying and deceit have no part in righteousness. It is significant that the law of the Old Covenant includes the commandment "*You shall not bear false witness against your neighbor.*" It is interesting to notice that in lying what God especially doesn't like outside of the fact that it is opposite to truth is that it deceives people, and so it doesn't honor them. Everything in God's heart is love and goodness toward His people. Lying is an offense to love.

Also, to walk in truth not only implies telling the truth or acting in the truth but also implies being real with one another. It often happens that some Christians hide a part of the truth, mainly because they think they need to protect themselves from others. To hide a part of the truth is actually lying. We are not supposed to tell everything to everybody, but in our relationships with others, the Bible exhorts us to be real and to practice "*love would be without hypocrisy.*" In the body of Christ, we know that we are all members of one another. We have all received the Holy Spirit, and we are the sons and daughters of God. This should lead us in a conduct that highly respects and honors our brothers and sisters whom Jesus died for. What we do to His body, we do for Jesus Himself; we are His family. Truth is a must in God's Kingdom. It is a column in His House.

To walk in truth is a way of life, and it is not only reserved for our relationships with God's people. As God's children, we were made to live like children of light everywhere we go. We are called to be the Light of the world, and to bring the Truth to the world. The Truth is Jesus who reconciles men with God the Father. Therefore, we cannot introduce Jesus and at the same time not walk in Truth.

To walk in Truth does not mean telling everything to everybody. But it is a conduct that manifests the Truth. We generally know in each situation what is needed to be said, revealed, or kept silent. If somebody confides a secret in us, this is obviously not something to share with others, even under the pretext of willing to be transparent. Sometimes, some situations require us to explain, witness, or clarify some facts or elements in order to keep unity. It is not always the case. We first live before God's eyes, and we are first true towards Him. Walking in truth before Him transports us in a dimension of freedom that exonerates us from having to justify ourselves for any of our actions. Walking in truth is more of a conduct that manifests God's light and truth. Most of the time, our attitude demonstrates the dimension of truth we live in better than our words.

There is no righteousness without truth.

Faithfulness

Faithfulness is an important aspect of righteousness because it means that we honor the fact that the people we interact with trust us. This is righteousness. Faithfulness is opposite to deception. When we show faithfulness, we don't deceive or disappoint. It is founded in love, and it is a fruit of the Spirit. We have seen that it is a part of holiness. There is nothing surprising in the fact that it is a part of righteousness too. In righteousness, faithfulness implies faithfulness toward God, His Word and principles, marriage, family, friendship, things that God entrusts us with, work, etc. It is rather rare to meet Christians who are faithful in all areas. Many of them are satisfied with themselves being faithful in marriage and at work, and they don't take seriously other areas such as supporting friends, or brothers and sisters in persecution, for example. Also in those kinds of situations we can demonstrate our faithfulness. This is righteousness. The Bible says that *"all who desire to live godly in Christ Jesus will suffer persecution"* (2 Timothy 3:12). We are then all exposed to persecution if we want to follow Jesus. We need one another in these difficult seasons of trials. These difficult times for our friends are opportunities to show them our faithfulness and love by helping them as it is given to us, and first of all by prayer. This is righteousness. It pleases God who has compassion for the contrite hearts and for those in affliction.

Respect

Righteousness involves respect as well. Respect of the rules, rights, laws, authorities, and people. The Bible teaches us to respect authorities, as they are all established by God. Authorities come with rules and laws, and we are supposed to observe them to make the society whole, to contribute to its peace, safety and prosperity. The law of the Old Testament was the first testament of Justice for Israel and was meant to grant wholeness in Israel as a people who served God and respected The Covenant between Him and them. Jesus Himself taught the people to *"render therefore to Caesar the things that are Caesar's, and to*

God the things that are God's." (Matthew 22:21). In the New Covenant, as reconciled children of God, we are taught to respect the authorities and laws of this world, as long as they don't enter into conflict with God's word. That is what Jesus meant when he said that, in respecting the rules of this world, we are not supposed to forget His word, His will, and His thought. His answer to the Pharisees teaches us to respect the authorities of this world, as well as honoring His Word. Nowadays, it can take a lot of creativity to be able respect at the same time the world's laws and God's Word. We are expected to seek a balance in all things, to be cautious and wise in following Him.

We know that at the end of times, Christians will be persecuted like never before. They will be put in jail simply because of their faith, and because the rules and laws of this world are becoming more and more opposed to God's Word.

Honor

Honoring our parents, the older generations, those who have been before us, people in general, is a part of righteousness. To honor our parents is the first command with a promise bound to it. It is something particularly important for God for us to honor our parents because He loves faithfulness toward those who have taken care of us, those who have been before us, but also because it reflects our faithfulness to God, who is our heavenly Father. If we don't honor our parents, how can we honor God that we don't see? It is like when John said, "*He who does not love his brother whom he has seen, how can he love God whom he has not seen?*" (1 John 4:20). Honor is a mix of faithfulness, loyalty, respect, care, attention, and paying tribute to someone. After God, our parents are the first ones we owe honor, in the biblical thought. We are supposed to love them, bless them, help them, honor who they are, and not despise them when they get old. This is an important aspect of righteousness.

The Bible teaches us to honor the old person. This is a part of righteousness as well, to respect and honor those who have been before us.

As sons and daughters of God, we are supposed to see the body of Christ as the household of God and to honor one another in our attitudes, words, and manners.

Honoring one's word is a way of honoring people as well. When we honor what we have promised, then we honor the person we have promised something to.

The Bible also exhorts us to honor all men and to pray for all men. This is also a part of righteousness for God who is the creator of all life, and who wants all men to be saved and reconciled with Him.

Good stewardship

Righteousness includes the way we manage or steward things or people that God entrusts us with. Money, businesses, or people under our influence or authority are good examples of areas in which we are expected to use righteousness and good stewardship.

Luke 16:11 "*Therefore, if you have not been faithful with the unrighteous mammon, who will commit to your trust the true riches? And if you have not been faithful in what is another's man, who will give you what is your own?*"

The way we steward money is an important element in righteousness because it is directly bound to the heart and the way we think. "*For where your treasure is, there your heart will be also.*" (Matthew 6:21). The way we behave with money reveals our hearts and the way we think. God's thought about money is abundance and prosperity for His children; a prosperity and abundance that comes from giving, and which purpose is giving. From a generous heart comes riches, and riches are for giving. Tithes and offerings are of course the most important way of giving, as it is reserved for God. Our faithfulness in tithes and offerings demonstrates our faith and love for God, as it determines our financial health. Giving to God's work in general also reflects our heart for God and His Kingdom. It contributes to our financial growth, as well as opens doors for abundant blessings in all areas: spiritual abundance, unlocked situations, material blessings, work, health, family, salvation of family members, etc.

Giving to God is the first element of righteousness is the financial area.

The second element of righteousness in the financial area is the good stewardship itself: to give to Caesar what is Caesar's, to God what is God's, and to people what belongs to people.

Another element of righteousness in finances, according to the Bible, is to enjoy it in the presence of God!

In **Deuteronomy 14:26**, the people who lived too far away from the place chosen by God for sacrifices were told to buy anything their heart desired to enjoy it in the Presence of The Lord. God loves celebrations and joy in His presence. He loves to see His children enjoy what He gave them.

As a leader, whether in business, at work, or in the church, the way we behave with people under our influence or authority also reveals our righteousness. If we have employees, we need to be careful not only to respect their legal rights but also to treat them with honor and respect. This notion of treating employees well is present in all the Old Testament and the Law, and it is very important to God's eye. The law included commandments about how to treat the servants, to preserve their rights and grant them a future and a hope to build their own house. After seven years of service, they were released with possessions and goods (herds, etc.) as a personal capital to start building their own house.

Some Christian leaders in business operate according to the world, pursuing prestige and financial increase to the detriment of their employees, minimizing or scoffing at their rights. It is actually oppression and the opposite of righteousness. God clearly disapproves of this, as we just saw with the example of the servants to whom were reserved a future and a hope.

Jeremiah 22:13 "*Woe to him who builds his house by unrighteousness and his chambers by injustice, who uses* *his neighbor's service without wages, and gives him nothing for his work."*

Our righteousness is also expected in our behavior with those under our responsibility, at work in general. For example, as a teacher, dealing with the youth demands effort and wisdom, and sometimes self-control, to edify, encourage, and influence them in the right way, rather than to discourage or humiliate. It is a part of righteousness to do all things as unto The Lord.

The leaders of the church are taught in the Bible to serve not as *"being lords over those entrusted to you, but being examples to the flock."* (1 Peter 5:3). We see here how righteousness is all together a matter of heart, attitudes, words, and actions.

We see that the components of righteousness mainly pertain to the character that is formed through the communion with The Lord. This character leads us into a conduct that reflects the heart of God for the people. Righteousness is then both the character and the conduct that manifests God's righteousness.

Called to walk in righteousness

Matthew 5:20 *"For I say to you that unless your*

righteousness exceeds the righteousness of the scribes and the Pharisees, you will by no means enter the kingdom of heaven."

2 Corinthians 5:21 *"God made Him who had no sin, to be sin for us, so that in Him we might become the righteousness of God."*

Psalm 23:3 *"He guides me along the right paths for His Name's sake."*

As God is righteous, we are called to be righteous. As Sons and Daughters of God, we are called to manifest the righteousness of God. Biblical righteousness is the only true righteousness, and the one that brings life. We cannot enter the kingdom of heaven unless we manifest His righteousness. It is then not an option but a standard we are called to live in.

Just like love and holiness, righteousness is a way to walk in, rather than a list of rules to observe.

In **Matthew 5:20**, we see that the law of the Old Testament is not sufficient to manifest righteousness according to God. We are supposed to manifest a righteousness that exceeds the righteousness of the scribes and the Pharisees. This righteousness can only come directly from God's heart. It is a righteousness that flows out from love. Therefore it is in the communion with the source of all love that we can manifest that kind of righteousness. From love comes our righteousness. Because we are loved by God, we can love Him. Because we love God, we can be righteous before Him, and because we love others, we can be righteous toward them.

Our righteousness is a powerful witness to the world. The world needs to see a generation that manifests a pure righteousness. Justice of the world fails become it is not founded in God's love. Righteousness without love is legalism or dead law, but true righteousness produces life. We are the salt and the light of the world, and it is our calling to show the heart of God in every aspect of life.

His Righteousness is grace and love

Righteousness according to God's heart has nothing to do with self- righteousness or self-justice. In the New Testament, there was a constant opposition between the righteousness that the scribes and the Pharisees were defending and what Jesus was teaching about righteousness. The Pharisees' righteousness was based on the obedience to the law of the Old Covenant and the feeling of self-righteousness that it provided to them. Their obedience to the law was mostly before men, and not an obedience of heart to please God; this is what Jesus disapproved of. Their self-righteousness was also reproved by Jesus who came and died to justify us, and who taught that only God justifies men.

Self-righteousness is believing that our actions justify us before God or men. There is pride, egocentrism, and rebellion toward God in this. A humble heart before God is needy and desiring of His justice in us.

Because of His Love, God manifested His justice toward us, which is absolute Grace. His Justice consists in having given Jesus to redeem our lives. The judgment for us was death, because of sin and because of the separation between us and God; but His justice was an amazing grace that allows us to live through the sacrifice of His Son. In the Old Testament, like in the New Testament, the term "justice" is generally associated to the idea of grace and love. It is because His righteousness is bound to His love, and His love manifests itself in grace. His justice is grace.

Psalm 145:17 "*The Lord is righteous in all His ways, gracious in all His works.*"

Psalm 33:5 "*The Lord loves righteousness and justice, the earth is full of His unfailing love.*"

1 John 3 : 10 *"This is how we know who the children of God are and who the children of the devil are: anyone who does not do what is right is not God's child, nor is anyone who does not love their brother and sister."*

If His righteousness is love and grace, we know then how to walk in righteousness. It is to manifest His love and His grace. If we love, we are honest, faithful, and we don't deceive. All the law is accomplished in love. If we love, then we don't lie. We give others what we owe them and we respect and honor them. We help them when they need it. If His righteousness is love and grace, then to manifest His righteousness goes beyond simply obeying the law and commandments. It is to manifest His love, His grace and compassion. This is why Jesus said that our righteousness must exceed the righteousness of the Pharisees.

Our love for God and for people determines our righteousness. From our love comes our righteousness. We can be righteous because we love God first and because we love others. Our righteousness is grace and compassion. We cannot deceive if we love people.

Jesus is our righteousness

2 Corinthians 5:21 *"God made Him who had no sin, to be* *sin for us, so that in Him we might become the righteousness of God."*

True righteousness comes from God's heart only. Jesus became our justice at the Cross. He justified us totally.

1 Corinthians 6:11 *"But you were washed, but you were sanctified, but you were justified in the name of The Lord Jesus, and by the Spirit of our God."*

Jesus is our justification, which means we are already considered as just and right by God Himself. Any actions, any good work, any service, or gift cannot make us more right than we already are through the blood of Jesus. We are seen as perfect in God's eyes, through Jesus who paid the price for our justification with His own life. Jesus is our righteousness.

This foundation places us in an amazing situation of rest concerning our righteousness. We know that whatever our actions are, no matter our mistakes or imperfections, God sees us as righteous anyway, as long as we don't intentionally sin. As long as our heart's desire is to honor and please Him, we are considered righteous. This foundation provides us a freedom and a rest that helps us effectively manifest His righteousness. It makes us love Him even more, understanding and realizing this freedom, which makes us grow even more in righteousness. The more we love Him, the more we are able to walk in His righteousness, which is founded in His love, and which is manifested in grace and love.

Our righteousness then is first a legal status through the Blood of Jesus. Then, it is an effective righteousness that comes from our love for God and communion with Him. In our communion with Him, He empowers us to be able to manifest His righteousness in all areas.

If true righteousness comes from the heart of God, we can only walk in it through a sincere communion with Him. It is a way we can walk in, in following Jesus and obeying the Holy Spirit.

Application

We learn a lot from reading the commandments of the Law of the Old Covenant, in the Old Testament, about principles of justice and righteousness according to God. They represent for us today examples and principles in His system of justice. But they represent only a pale frame of what is true righteousness according to His heart, which is revealed in Jesus only. True righteousness is righteousness that comes from His love, and we can only manifest this if we remain in communion with Him. It is then a way we walk in as we follow Him and remain in Him. In all areas, we can manifest His righteousness by hearing the Holy Spirit.

In some situations, it is not that obvious to know what is right. But love will always determine what is right. It will always reveal what should be done, because His righteousness is love and grace. When we don't know what to do, then grace is always the best response because it is actually how God manifests His justice toward us.

Love and grace are the foundations of righteousness, as well as its demonstration. We cannot walk in true righteousness unless we walk in love. Only the communion with God can build in us a true character of integrity that demonstrates His righteousness. As with love, righteousness is a way we are called to walk in, following Jesus and remaining in His love.

Activation

1-Is there an area of righteousness that you feel you should develop, whether in character or in conduct?

2-Take a moment in the Presence of God to bring Him this area. Thank Him for the fact you are justified through the blood of Jesus. Repent for inadequacy with His righteousness in this area. And ask God to replace it with His righteousness. Thank Him that it is done as you ask Him; it has already been assured to you at the Cross.

3-As practice or reeducation of this area, each time you find yourself in a situation where you must face this area, think about the fact you have already received the empowerment that you need, because of your prayer and confession, that you are already transformed by the law of the Holy Spirit who lives in you. Think that you have been transformed by the victory of Jesus at the Cross, and that you only have to manifest it now.

4-If you fail at first, don't be discouraged the next time, and start again to manifest God's righteousness in that area. This is sometimes a question of training and repetition. You must learn to change your habits in that area, but the victory is already granted for you. Continue to thank God and worship Him for His victory.

5-Think now about a situation you are/were in where you don't/didn't know what is right and what to do.

6- Spend a moment with God and start to bless the people involved in the situation. Ask God to give you love for these people, and to help you see the situation as He sees it.

7- Identify now the aspects of the situation that you can change according to His righteousness. As much as it depends on you, make the changes according to what is right.

4 WAY OF TRUTH

Revelation 15:3 *"... great and marvelous are your works, Lord God Almighty! Just and true are your ways, Oh King of the saints!"*

Psalm 25:10 *"All the paths of The Lord are mercy and Truth, to such as keep His covenant and His testimonies."*

Truth is another foundation in God's Kingdom. It is a way of God: as He is truth, everything He does is truth. All His ways are truth. We cannot enter the kingdom of Heaven unless we walk in the Truth.

We live in a world of confusion and blindness where truth

only represents what people feel or desire. People's desires, emotions, or experiences represent what is true to them. Only a few people really seek the truth. But truth is not something subjective as this world tends to believe. Truth is a reality, it is unique, and its source is a person. This person is Jesus. And God wants every man to know the truth and be reconciled with Him.

What is truth?

If we asked anyone to give a definition of what truth is, we would have as many answers as persons who answer the question. This world has so rejected the truth that it has become an abstract concept that is changing and subjective.

The question "*What is truth?*" was posed by Pontius Pilate to Jesus before His crucifixion, when Jesus said, "*I came to the world to testify to the truth.*" His question was cynical and reflects how little the world is concerned about the truth, and how it is considered as a vague and subjective notion.

However, the Bible only gives a clear and precise meaning of what truth is. Truth in the Bible always represents God and all that refers to Him. We can define it as all that refers to God: His being, His Person, His will, His character, His ways and His works. He is Truth, and so Truth is the expression of God Himself. In the Bible, the word "truth" serves many times to denote God Himself, as well as His Word. Because the definition of truth is bound to who God is, truth is a spiritual reality first. It is a theological definition first.

The word "truth" in the Bible serves also to denote what is real, or to express that things really are. This is a second definition of truth drawn from the Word of God. But we know that reality exists because God declared it and made it so. God is the source and the creator of all reality. Therefore, truth is the manifestation or expression of God. It is His existence, and everything that comes from Him: His will, His word, and His works.

Jesus is Truth

John 14:6 "*I am the way, the truth, and the life. No one comes to the Father except through Me.*"

John 8:32 "*And you shall know the truth, and the truth shall make you free.*"

Before anything else, truth is a person, and this person is Jesus. He is Truth, and He is the source of all that is true. He is what is true, so everything that is true is an expression of who He is.

What does it exactly mean that Jesus is Truth? When Jesus said, "*I am the truth,*" He first established that there is only one truth. There is only one truth that all humanity longs to know without knowing what it is. The meaning of life, the existence of God and who He is, the purpose and the destiny of mankind – every answer is included in this unique truth. Men seek all their lives in many different directions, hoping to find a truth, but there is a unique truth that answers to all these universal questions, and this truth is Jesus, who came to reconcile men with the only true God.

There is a second statement included in this declaration of Jesus – truth does exist, and it is God Himself, who came on earth to redeem all men from sin and death and to reconcile them with God The Father. The Truth responds to any emptiness in the heart of men, to their need to be reconciled with their creator, the source of all life.

There is a third statement included in this declaration: Truth is a person, and this person is Jesus. Therefore, if we want to know the Truth, we need to come to Him. Not only is He the truth that all humanity longs for, but He is also the truth for any situation that needs clarity.

Jesus is the very and ultimate expression of God. This is

also means that He is the Truth. In the world, many religions, doctrines or philosophies claim to speak or possess the truth, but the only Truth is God, who, because of His love, sent His only Son to redeem us from sin and death: it is Jesus. The only truth is Jesus.

Jesus, during His ministry on earth, revealed God to people. The Gospel of John continually shows us that Jesus reveals God to mankind (1 John 1:18). When His disciples asked Him to show them the Father, He answered them that they saw the Father in Him. He said that He and The Father are one. Jesus does the works of God and speaks the very words of God. To see and know Jesus is to see and know God.

How do we know that we know Jesus? The Bible says that we know Him and we remain in Him when we abide in His word. But when we come to His word, we need to come to seek Him, and not to seek a set of truths about Him.

Jesus is God, who reveals Himself in His word. He is the very truth that every man needs to know to understand his purpose, to fulfill his destiny, to be reconciled with His creator and receive true abundant life for eternity.

His word is the Truth

John 17:17 *"Sanctify them by your truth. Your word is truth."*

Psalm 119:160 *"The entirety of your word is truth, and every one of your righteous judgments endures forever."*

As God is truth, everything that He speaks is truth as well. Therefore, His word is truth. The whole Bible is inspired by God and is true from the beginning to the end. God cannot lie, and what He speaks, He accomplishes it. He doesn't repent or change His mind when He declares something. His word is a living word that produces life by the Holy Spirit. It is the expression of His heart to His people, and the explanation of His plan for humanity, for anyone who wants to know the truth.

The Bible is true at all levels: historical, scientific, prophetic, moral, and spiritual.

The historical accuracy of the Scriptures is abundantly demonstrated by archeological discoveries. Archeological confirmations of the Bible are innumerable, especially in the last century, and an attentive reading of the Bible has even led to some amazing archeological discoveries.

The scientific accuracy is proved in the fact that many principles of modern science are given as evident in the Bible, long before they were experimented and adopted by scientists. Among those principles, we can find: the roundness of the Earth (Isaiah 40:22), the vast number of stars (Jeremiah 33:22), the gravitational field (Job 26:7), the essential function of blood in the life process (Leviticus 17:11), the almost infinite extent of the universe (Isaiah 55:9), and many others.

The Bible manifests remarkable prophetic evidence. Hundreds of biblical prophecies have been fulfilled, often long after the period they were spoken. For example, Daniel prophesied in about 548 BC the coming of Christ as the promised savior of Israël, 483 years after the Persian King would allow Israel to rebuild Jerusalem which was in ruins. This prophecy was fulfilled in its terms, several hundreds of years later. There are innumerable prophecies about nations, cities, the course of history, the spread of the Gospel, the change in men's behavior, etc. that have already been fulfilled. The prophetic dimension of the Bible confirms that this book is the Word of God, and it is the truth.

On a moral and spiritual level, the Bible gives principles which are open doors for blessings, prosperity and happiness. Practicing them is the best way to notice that these principles work and are true. They mainly consist in loving, honoring, and giving. These moral and spiritual dimensions of the Bible also confirm that The Bible is true, and that the principles that it teaches are true and effective.

Another piece of evidence that the Bible is truth is the testimony of multitudes of people who have believed it, and who have experienced that its promises and council are true, and that its wonderful message of salvation meets every need in men's hearts.

As Jesus is the Truth, The Bible is His word and confirms the Truth. The consistent theme of the Bible from the beginning to the end is the great work of God in the creation and the redemption of all things, through His only Son, Jesus Christ. Everything in the Bible is meant to introduce Jesus.

The Holy Spirit is truth

John 16:13 *"However, when He, the Spirit of truth has come, He will guide you into all truth; for He will not speak on His own authority, but whatever He hears He will speak; and He will tell you things to come."*

Psalm 51:6 *"Behold, you desire truth in the inward parts, and in the hidden part you will make me to know wisdom."*

As a Person of the Trinity, the Holy Spirit is truth. The Holy

Spirit is one with the Father and Jesus. The three are one. The Holy Spirit is called the "spirit of truth" because He is the Spirit of God, who is Truth, and because He speaks the truth about the Father, Jesus, and about everything that God wants to reveal to us. He is also the one who opens the scriptures to us, who witnesses the truth in prophecies, who reveals to us things to come, who leads us, and who guides us in all the truth. He is the Spirit of God in us who enlighten us, who shows us where to walk, what to speak and what to do when we need it.

In our communion with God, the Holy Spirit has a fundamental part. He is always with us; He is the helper, the comforter, and the revealer of the Father's will and heart.

His ways are truth

Revelation 15:3 "... *great and marvelous are your works, Lord God Almighty! Just and true are your ways, Oh King of the saints!*"

If Jesus is Truth, everything that He does, all His works and all His ways are true. Not only His works, but the way He is, and the way He operates things are true. When we speak of works, we often speak of things that have already been accomplished or fulfilled. We can easily say then that God's works are true, because we can directly see their accomplishment. But when we speak of His ways, we often mean the way He is, or the way He operates things. It deals more with the process of doing things than the works themselves. In that case, we understand that we need to be assured that His ways are also truth. In the process, while the Lord is doing things in our lives, we can lose patience, we can doubt, or get discouraged by obstacles or time. We need to know that His ways, His processes are true and come to full accomplishment.

His ways are directly bound to His character and His person. We have explored so far some of God's ways: Love, Holiness, Righteousness, and Truth. As He calls us to walk in His ways, He grants us that His ways are true and we can trust them. If we rely on Him and follow His ways, He assures us that we won't be confused. We won't be deceived in following His ways, because they are true; they are the true way of victory and success. The Bible exhorts us to "*not be conformed to this world, but be transformed by the renewing of -our- mind, that -we- may prove what is that good, and acceptable and perfect will of God.*" (Romans 12:2). This world of sin would naturally push us to walk in the opposite of God's ways: indifference, selfishness, self-ambition, self-righteousness, etc., and walking in God's ways can sometimes seem to be a challenge. We can have the feeling of swimming against the current, but God assures us that His ways are true, and that they won't fail. We are granted to walk in victory, and to be more than conquerors if we follow His ways.

Called to walk in the truth

Truth is not only a way of God, but Jesus Himself is the personification of truth; therefore, we are called to walk in the truth. We cannot say we love God if we don't walk in the truth. He is truth, so if we love Him, we love truth. To walk in the truth, we know now that we need to follow Jesus, to remain in His word and to walk in His ways. If Jesus is truth, we are supposed to manifest the truth. The world around us needs to see the truth through us. We are called to be ambassadors of the truth.

Walk according to His word

The Word of God is truth because it entirely expresses God's love for mankind and announces His plan of redemption and salvation through Jesus. All the biblical stories converge on this main truth: Jesus is the gift of love of God, to save and reconcile the world to Himself. This is why the Bible is truth; it is God's word and so it cannot lie. It witnesses of the Truth, who is Jesus.

If we want to walk in the truth, we then need first to seek God in His word. God can be found first in His Word. The Bible is not to be read like a novel or any other book. It is a living book, and if we read it with the Holy Spirit, it has the power of transforming us.

Hebrews 4:12 *"For the Word of God is living and powerful, and sharper than any two-edged sword, piercing even to the division of soul and spirit, and of joints and marrow, and is a discerner of the thoughts and intents of the heart."*

God always wants to speak to us through His Word. He always will speak to us in His word, as long as we come with the intention of meeting Him in His word. As Christians, we have received the Holy Spirit, who opens the Scriptures to us and aligns our reading with His meaning and purpose. *"The letter kills, but the Spirit gives life."* (2 Corinthians 3:6). If we read the Bible with the Holy Spirit, we receive it in truth, as we are supposed to receive it. There are not multiple possible interpretations for the Bible, but only one Holy Spirit who shows us and makes us understand the Truth.

As the Bible is truth, anyone who comes to read it with the

intention of meeting God will always find the Truth. Therefore, any non-believer who sincerely desires to know the Truth and comes to read the Bible, will also find the truth because the Word will never return where it came from without any effect.

Also, the entirety of the Word is truth, so we cannot isolate some portions and exclude some others, according to our own perceptions, experiences, desires or intentions, if we truly want to be led by God's word. We cannot pretend to walk according to His word if we make a selection or an interpretation of it. The whole Bible is the truth, so we need to receive it in its wholeness.

The Word of God teaches us, instructs us, leads us and shows us how to walk in our Christian walk. It is our lamp for us to know how to walk. It gives many principles and ways that as Christians we are supposed to walk in. It gives us a main conduct to follow for our lives. But reading it once is not sufficient to be able to live the lives we are supposed to live as children of God. Otherwise, it is religion or a simple doctrine we follow. If we want to walk according to His word, we need to continually feed ourselves, meditate, and remain in His word. In our daily walk, we need God's direction, encouragement, word, etc. This is why we need to come to Him daily in His word, expecting Him to personally speak to us. It's a part of our communion with Him to come to seek Him in His word, and to let Him speak to us directly and personally. Therefore, walking according to His Word is not only following the principles and ways that the Bible teaches but also following what God speaks to us personally day after day. The word of God is the foundation of our relationship with Him. He is the center in our meditation of the scriptures, and we need to be open to what He wants to speak to us personally each time we read them. This is how He can lead us to walk in the truth, through His word.

To follow Jesus

To walk in the truth obviously implies to follow Jesus, as He is The Truth. To follow Jesus, we need to know Him personally. We need to have a personal relationship with Him. We have seen that He first reveals Himself in His word, and so knowing Him implies knowing Him in His word, but He also has multiple ways to manifest Him to us. If we want to know God, we need to spend time with Him and seek Him. He can speak to us in many ways, and He declares that His sheep can hear His voice. We were created in His image; therefore, we know that God speaks, hears, is alive and loves His children. He is gracious and wants the best for us. We can come at any time before His throne of grace and be real with Him. This is exactly what He likes: to see His children trust Him, rely on Him and be real with Him in a communion of love. The Bible invites us to put before Him our requests, to express to Him our demands and needs.

Our communion with God grows with the time we spend in His Presence, with the quality of our intimacy with Him, with the sincerity of our heart when coming to Him. It changes and gets deeper and deeper as we know Him more and more, as we experience His faithfulness and unfailing love. There is not a unique form in our relationship with God, as we all are different, and even our own relationship with Him changes with seasons and maturity. But our communion with God generally implies acts of thankfulness, various forms of worship and praise, conversations, supplications, confidence, prophetic actions or acts of faith, etc. God also has many ways to answer us or speak to us, which we will explore later in this book.

To know Jesus, to remain in a real communion with Him, is the sine qua non condition to follow Him. How can we follow Him if we don't know Him? We need to know what He thinks and what He says about our lives if we want to follow His council and let Him walk before us.

There are circumstances or seasons when following Jesus looks like a narrow path where everything around us seems to be opposed and hostile to us. In those seasons, everything seems to tell us that we are not on the right path, because all things are opposite to what we believe and to the vision we follow. But those circumstances and oppositions are not the truth. They are lies and delusions to make our vision blur. Most of the weapons of the enemy of our souls are lies, because he is a liar. But if we know, by our communion with Him, we are following Jesus, then we know we are walking in the truth. Jesus is the truth, so the best way to be sure we walk in the truth is to keep in communion with Him. He says that his sheep hear His voice. We are the flock of His pasture, so He is able to lead us, guide us, and guard us on His path, as long as we voluntarily remain under His covering and keep the communion with Him.

Following Jesus can imply walking in a different or surprising way sometimes. Because God is a God of creativity, He likes to lead us into new initiatives for the advancement of His Kingdom on Earth. Pioneer work, new forms of evangelism, or service, can find us in the middle of such opposition that the vision we walk in can sometimes seem unreal and unreachable. But in pursuing this vision, each step we take is more real and true than any form of opposition as opposition is founded on a lie. We walk in victory, and the vision we are pursuing is more real than the material world. Everything that came from the heart of God is always more real and true than any strategy of the enemy to discourage us and dissuade us fro pursuing the vision because any weapon formed by the enemy is based on lies, as he is the father of lies.

As long as we know we follow Jesus, we know we walk in the truth. We know we follow Jesus when we walk according to His Word, when we are in a true relationship with Him where He speaks to us and we let Him minister to us, change us, rule over us, and lead us.

Walk in His ways

Psalm 25:10 *"All the paths of The Lord are mercy and Truth."*

The ways of God are true. We are meant to walk in all His ways if we follow God. His ways are true, meaning that they are powerful and they lead us in truth to the fulfillment of what we pursue as we follow them. They don't deceive. They are right and sure. For example, when we walk in love, we sow love and therefore we receive love because God promises us that he who gives receives. When we walk in love, we operate in the most powerful way that can be. Love is powerful. Nothing can resist love. When Jesus teaches us to love our enemies, he knows that our enemies need His love and that once they enter in contact with His love, they can change and become the people they were meant to be. He knows that love has the power of changing our enemies into our best supports.

God's ways are powerful and true. If we walk in the truth, we know that the truth has the power to set us free. Truth opens the door of freedom. *"And you shall know the truth, and truth will make you free."* (John 8:32). Walking in the ways of God is always a gain and never a loss. It always leads us in victory. To walk in His ways is to walk after Him, to imitate what He does and how He does it, to adopt His nature and behave according to His character.

The communion with God makes us know Him more and more. The more we know Him, the more we understand His ways, and the more walking in His ways becomes natural and easy to us.

Be real with one another.

Ephesians 4:25 *"Therefore, putting away lying, let each* *one of you speak truth with His neighbor, for we are members of one another."*

A part of walking in the truth consists in being real with one another. Obviously, lying has nothing to do with the children of God. Not being real with one another is actually lying; many Christians are not really aware of that. Many Christians think that because they don't directly lie (or say something that they know is wrong), they don't lie if they hide something or pretend something that is not entirely true. Oftentimes, some Christians pretend to be well, to be happy, when they are unhappy and in distress. Lying is lying, and truth is truth though. Not being real with one another is lying, because it is pretending something that is not true. Oftentimes, Christians that are not real try to hide their fears, their worry, their feelings or emotions. Sometimes they hide situations out of fear of being judged by others.

If the Bible invites us to be real with one another, it is because we are members of one another, and we need one another. We are supposed to confess our sins to one another because it is a powerful way to take a position against them. When we confess our sins to brothers in Christ, we confess them before the Holy Spirit in them and before the spiritual authorities as an act of reconciliation.

We are the Body of Christ and we are called to rule with Jesus in eternity. Lying has no place in our lives.

We have everything to gain in being real with one another, because everything we need is in the body of Christ, to council us, support us, pray and intercede with us, comfort us, etc. We are the family of God. We are not supposed to say everything to anybody, but God gives us wisdom to see with whom we can share what.

Manifest the truth to the world

We are called to be ambassadors of the Truth, who is Jesus. Before spreading the Gospel, the testimony of our lives and behavior is eloquent. It is only through the communion with our dear Lord that we can manifest who He is and walk in His ways. Our character like His, our walk conformed to His ways, our love manifesting His heart – these are the best ways of manifesting the truth to the world. Jesus said that it is through the love we have for one another that the world will know that we are His disciples. The truth is manifested to the world through the manifestation of His ways: love, righteousness, holiness, truth, peace, etc.

This world needs to see a generation that manifests His

love and all that He is. We can manifest the Truth only if we follow Him and His ways. We make God lie if we preach the Gospel but don't truly follow Him and walk in His ways. The spreading of the Gospel needs to be confirmed by a living testimony of who He is, through our lives and ways. We become one with Him, if we remain in a true communion with Him. Our thoughts, emotions, visions, and actions become in alignment with His, and this is how people can see Him through us.

Application

First of all, Jesus Himself represents the truth that all men seek. He is Truth, and if we want to know the truth, we need to know Him. We understand all the truth in contemplating Him, in observing Him and His ways. Truth is a fundamental way in His kingdom; it is present in all that He speaks, all that He does, and in all His ways. All those who are called by His purpose cannot love Him if they don't love the truth. To know God implies loving the truth.

We are called to manifest the truth, who is Jesus Himself. To walk after Him, according to His character, His love, His will, His ways, and His word is to manifest the truth. We become one with Him when we remain in a true communion with Him, when we remain in His word, and this is how we can naturally and easily manifest Him.

Activation

Take a moment in the Presence of God and ask Him to show you:

1- Is there an aspect of your life where you think you don't manifest the truth?

2- What do you think you should do to manifest the truth in that area?

3- How do you evaluate your ability to be real with others?

4- What do you think you should do to improve your ability to be real with others?

5 WAY OF PEACE- REST

Romans 8:6 *"For to be carnally minded is death, but to be spiritually minded is life and peace."*

Romans 3:17 *"The way of peace they have not known..."*

God is a God of peace. Innumerable are the verses in the Bible that speak about God's peace. Jesus is called the Prince of Peace. Peace is a full component of God's kingdom. It is a way of God we are called to walk in.

Peace concerns two main aspects: being and remaining in the Lord's peace, and being an ambassador of His peace. Jesus Himself manifested the two aspects of Peace during

His ministry on Earth. He was Himself in complete peace in the worst circumstances, and He deposited peace to anyone He ministered to. Let's remember the crossing of the rough sea, when the disciples were crying for help thinking they were dying while Jesus was soundly sleeping. He was continually in peace. Then He commanded peace to the elements, and suddenly everything was calm. Jesus often gave words of consolation and peace to people He met. He often spoke words like "be in peace," "don't worry," "fear not," etc. The words He spoke were effective to immediately transform hearts and bring peace.

As children of the God of peace, this is what we are called to live as well. We are called to live in His peace in all circumstances, as well as to manifest and bring His peace to people around us.

The God of peace

Isaiah 52:7 *"How beautiful upon the mountains, are the feet of him who brings good news; who proclaims peace, who brings glad tidings of good things, who proclaim salvation, who says to Zion, your God reigns!"*

It is interesting to think that God is all together powerful and omnipotent. He is the God of Hosts, but He is a God of

Peace. That is what makes Him God and unique. He loves peace. Jesus as the Prince of Peace means that His kingdom is a kingdom of peace, and that peace is a witness of who He is.

The ultimate purpose of God is to see His children live the fullness of all that they were meant to live from the beginning of the world – to live in perfect harmony with Him and with one another in love, joy, and abundant life. This is what constitutes the idea of peace in the Bible.

Peace is first an inner state of wellness that is not troubled by any inner turmoil, sin or circumstance. It is an inner wellness that comes from our communion with God. Without God, there is no peace. He is the only one who provides peace. Medical reports confirm that 80 % of diseases are bound to inner conflicts like stress, fear, worry, and hate. The Bible says that in the end of times, there will be wars, and people will be rebellious and hostile. It shows how much this world needs to know the true peace that only Jesus can give.

In Hebrew the word for peace is "shalom." That contains the idea of total wellness, happiness, prosperity, and success in all areas. There is also the idea of "reconciliation" included in the term "peace." These are the two dimensions of peace that we are called to live: wellness, inner happiness that comes from a communion with the God of peace, and peace in our relationship with others.

Jesus manifests those two dimensions. As God, He is peace and the provider of peace, and He is in perfect harmony with the Father, as He is one with Him.

His peace is manifested in His presence. His presence is always a presence of peace. When He speaks to us, we know it's Him through the peace that overwhelms us. We also know that we remain in Him through the peace we have. Peace is always a mark of His presence and that we are walking on the right path.

When Jesus appeared to some of His servants in the Old Testament, He often said to them *"shalom"* because He knows how easily men can be enveloped by fear. Peace always walks with Him. He is the source of true peace.

What is God's peace?

God gives us His peace. His peace comes to dwell in our hearts when we enter in a trustful relationship with our heavenly Father. True peace only comes from reconciliation with our heavenly Father, because it is only through the communion with the author of our lives that we can be in total harmony with who we are and with others.

As children of God, our peace doesn't depend on circumstances. Our peace resides in the fact we are sons and daughters of the Almighty God, that He has adopted us forever, that we are loved by Him and that He is pleased with us.

Philippians 4:7 *"And the peace of God which surpasses all understanding, will guard your hearts and minds through Christ Jesus."*

John 14:27 *"Peace I leave you. My peace I give to you; not as the world gives do I give to you. Let not your heart be troubled, neither let it be afraid."*

God's peace has nothing to do with an earthly peace. An earthly peace is only apparent, and temporary, as we know we live in a world of iniquity. People who don't know God and affirm that they are in peace forget most of time the fears, anxieties, worries or turmoil that inhabit them, because these have become a part of them. They speak about a temporary and a superficial feeling that they have the impression of having most of time.

God's peace is supernatural, profound, abundant and overwhelming. It cannot be shaken. It is strong like a river. Peace is compared to a river in the Bible. (Isaiah 48:18).

This is an interesting comparison as a river contains several characteristics. First, there is a notion of power in a river. A river can produce energy (electricity, etc.), and its stream is a force in itself. It speaks about the power of peace. Peace is a power in itself; it represents stability, consistency, a dam against any kind of fear or trouble. There is a notion of plenitude as well in a river. A river represents an abundant reserve of water. God's peace has nothing to do with a small peace. It is abundant, deep and overwhelming. A river represents life as well. Cities were often built next to rivers because of their supply of water, food, irrigation, etc. – all that allows life to multiply. It is the same with peace; it allows prosperity in life, prosperity of the soul, and it makes life and relationships easier.

God's peace establishes itself in us when we come to Jesus, through the gift of the Holy Spirit. Peace is actually a fruit of the Spirit. It also means that it can grow. Our peace can be multiplied. It is a fruit that can be developed as our communion with the God of Peace grows.

There is an important correlation between peace and the other ways of God that we need to be aware of. Peace is always in interaction with other activities of the Holy Spirit:

1- Peace and love

2 Corinthians 13:11 *"Finally brethren, farewell. Become complete. Be of good comfort, be one of mind; live in peace, and the God of love and peace will be with you."*

There is an obvious and deep correlation between peace and love. Love is manifested in unity and peace. Peace is the binding that preserves love.

2- Peace and holiness

1 Thessalonians 5:23 *"Now may The God of peace Himself sanctify you completely, and may your whole spirit, soul and body be preserved blameless at the coming of our Lord Jesus Christ."*

Peace is first a big part of holiness. It is also the ground of our sanctification. We have received peace through Jesus. He is our sanctification, which enables us to walk with confidence in holiness. Peace empowers us to make our election of children of God sure.

3- Peace and righteousness

James 3:18 *"Now the fruit of righteousness is sown in peace by those who make peace."*

The ground to do the works of righteousness of the Holy Spirit is peace. It is the binding we seek to preserve all works of righteousness. Any work of righteousness is meant to spread peace and love.

4- Peace and grace

Revelations 1:4 "*Grace to you and peace from Him who is, and who was and who is to come.*"

Grace is an undeserved favor from God to us. It is His free gift. Grace empowers us to do God's will and is the only means of reconciliation with our Father. Grace leads us to peace. Without grace, no peace is possible.

5- Peace and faith

Isaiah 26:3 "*You will keep him in perfect peace, whose mind is stayed on you, because he trusts in you.*" Keeping our eyes on Jesus with trust and confidence is a key for peace. Faith produces peace. And peace strengthens our faith.

6- Peace and life

Romans 8:6 *"For to be carnally minded is death, but to be spiritually minded is life and peace."*

Obedience to the Holy Spirit produces life and peace. We can only find true peace in the communion with the God of life and peace. This communion gives us access to eternal and abundant life. We have peace, being assured of our destination in eternity and enjoying His abundant life on Earth. Also tasting His abundant life here on Earth contributes to making our peace grow. Peace opens up access to the life of the Spirit and makes life easier in general, as life of the Spirit is a key for peace.

There are two possible applications of His peace in us. The first one is to know and to live His peace for ourselves, and the second one is to be able to manifest His peace in our relationship with others.

To dwell in His peace

Psalm 37:11 *"But the meek shall inherit the earth, and shall delight themselves in the abundance of peace."*

Isaiah 32:18 *"My people will dwell in a peaceful habitation, in secure dwellings, and in quiet resting place."*

This is the heart of the Father, for His sons and daughters to live this abundant peace that He has in store for them. It is His heart to let us know the riches of His love that are infinite and unlimited. As His children, He often speaks about us as His flock, His sheep, in His word. He likes this image because it represents well the tenderness of the shepherd for his sheep; he leads them in a green and quiet pasture. This image represents well the peace that resides in trusting the Great Shepherd. He is the one who leads our life, who provides for us, who guides and protects us; and in this life of total surrendering, we have nothing to fear.

Peace is a fruit of the Spirit. It means that the more we grow in the communion with the Holy Spirit, the more our peace grows. We have seen that peace is like a river; therefore, it continually flows. It is in remaining in His love, in His presence that we can experience a continual flow of peace in our lives. God's peace is real. It is not something we can make by ourselves. It is a free gift that flows from the communion with Him. We freely receive it by grace.

We have seen that our peace comes first from being reconciled with our Creator through Jesus. Yes, redemption and salvation in Jesus provides a peace that nothing can be compared with. But then if we want to experience a continual peace that flows like a river, we need to dwell in His presence continually. Because His presence is peace.

In His presence, we find peace and rest. He is the Prince of Peace, and therefore if we want to be in continual peace, we need to remain in His presence continually. There is nothing like His presence, which provides all together love, restoration, peace, joy and consolation.

There is also a key for peace in growing in the knowledge of Him. The more we know Him, the more we trust Him as we experience His faithfulness. It provides peace.

The more we know Him, the more we are able to walk and remain in His peace, in all kind of circumstances. The enemy of our souls will always try to steal our peace because he knows this is a demonstration of our faith, which is precious to God. Therefore, remaining in peace in spite of circumstances or oppositions confirms our faith and our trust in God.

To remain in His rest

Rest is very important for God. This notion has been present since the Creation when it was said that God rested on the seventh day from all His work. (Genesis 2:2). God was not tired, He never is. He didn't rest. But in this notion of rest, there is the idea of enjoying life. He simply enjoyed and appreciated what He had just created. He had just created what was meant to be the most delightful pleasure of His: a people who would be His family and a world for them to take care of. The masterpiece and the climax of the creation was when He created men. He said He created them in His image and designed the whole creation for men to be in their possession and to be subject to them. After that, it was natural for Him to take a pause and admire the beauty of what He had just designed, to rejoice and enjoy it. This is the first definition of what rest means to Him: to rejoice and to enjoy the life He gives us. God gave us a life to enjoy it. For many reasons, we often tend to forget it, but the first purpose of life, as children of God, is to enjoy life!

In the beginning of creation, Adam and Eve were in the garden, simply enjoying life and the beauty of the creation. They didn't have to work to produce food or to earn anything. Everything was a gift from God for them to enjoy. They didn't need any clothes or any vehicle, as they were living in the supernatural realm of God. It is not said, but we could easily imagine that they were transported wherever they wanted to be, as they lived in such a proximity with God. They could stand in the very presence of God, as it is said that God enjoyed coming and walking in the Garden of Eden. They were designed to enjoy life, to rule over the garden, and to multiply! What a wonderful life!

The first purpose of God for us in creating us is to enjoy life. It is fundamental to understand that to not miss it. Today, if life doesn't look like it was in Eden, we still have a life with the first purpose to enjoy it. In today's world, we must work to live and confront a world that doesn't know God, which can make life more challenging. But the purpose of God in giving life to us is still the same as it was in the beginning of the creation; He wants us to enjoy our life. There are always things in our lives that we can enjoy, even if we don't always live all that we would like to live. Because God is good and everything works for our good.

Now, God knows His children. He is a God of love and wisdom. He knows how He made us and knows that men need a purpose in life to accomplish. He knows He planted in the heart of men a sense of destiny and purpose. He is a God of destiny and purpose. And He does have a plan and purpose for each of us. He knows men need to feel useful and find true happiness in accomplishing the purpose they were meant for.

This is how we can truly enjoy life today, in walking in His very purpose for us, contributing to the advancement of His kingdom on Earth. This is actually what provides the greatest joy and satisfaction – fulfilling the plan He has for us in helping the growth of His Kingdom on Earth. It is actually a part of enjoying life.

The second meaning of rest according to the Bible is trusting Him in everything. In all our works, we are supposed to rest in Him. It means to let Him do His part and only do what He asks us to do. Rest is supposed to be a part of all that we do. Even in our relationship with others, rest must be at the first place, to let the Holy Spirit do His part.

When we rest in Him in all that we do, we let the Holy Spirit do His job to perfect what we do. Rest is an attitude of continual surrendering to God in all that we do. It has nothing to do with passivity, but it is an active collaboration with the Holy Spirit to let Him work in all our situations. It is an attitude of resting in Him. There is always a benefit in letting Him do His part in everything we put our hands on. This can only be done through a true communion with Him. As our communion with Him grows, He shows us what to do and what to say in every situation, and He intervenes to support and confirm what we do or say. We are sons and daughters of God. Any of our actions and words are significant for this world and for the body of Christ. We have an impact in what we do, whether we are aware of it or not. This is also why God gives us His Spirit, to manifest His Spirit in this world.

We are called to live His rest – to enjoy the life He gave us, in accomplishing His purpose as well as resting on Him in all that we do, trusting Him to perfect our actions and operate in His powerful and decisive part.

It is a continual rest that we are called to live. This is part of what the way of peace is. Rest is very closely related to peace. To walk in peace includes walking in rest. Rest is privileged ground for peace. It is closely associated to faith, and then provides access to peace.

Called to manifest His peace

Matthew 5:9 *"Blessed are the peacemakers, for they shall be called sons of God."*

We are ambassadors of His peace. We have been given the ministry of reconciliation. It means that as Christians we are supposed to introduce Jesus to the world. He reconciles us with the Father and brings God's presence wherever we go. His presence includes His peace.

If we live His peace, if we dwell and remain in it, it is much easier to manifest His peace in our relationships with others.

When we have learned to cultivate God's presence and peace in our lives, then the same peace is ready to flow in our relationships with others, whatever the circumstances may look like.

In all our relationships, peace is supposed to be a mark of our walk with Jesus and of the communion with His Spirit. Peace is a fruit of the Spirit. The more we grow in the communion with the Prince of Peace, the more our peace can be manifested in all our relationships and in all circumstances.

Our presence is supposed to bring God's presence and peace everywhere we go. We are His temple, He lives in us, and His peace is supposed to flow through us if we let Him rule in us. People can feel God's presence and peace through us. As a teacher, I can witness how my students who don't know God feel His presence and peace during my classes. They are overwhelmed, and I can see them being enveloped in His presence and Peace. Oftentimes, they like to stay after class, continuing to ask questions. It is like they don't want to leave this place of peace.

Peace is a way we are called to walk in, in everything. As children of God, peace is supposed to characterize us in all that we do, in our apprehension of events and circumstances, and in our relationship with others.

Called to be peacemakers

We are not only called to walk in God's peace and to manifest God's peace, but to be peacemakers. Our peace can also be demonstrated in our ability to create peace around us.

Peace through righteousness

Psalm 34:14 *"Depart from evil and do good. Seek peace and pursue it."*

How can we seek peace and pursue peace? Do good. Seek your neighbor's interest and not yours only. Love your neighbor like yourself.

Psalm 72:3 *"The mountains will bring peace to the people, and the little hills, by righteousness."*

Righteousness is a bridge for peace. We have seen how righteousness is correlated with grace and love in God's thought. Because God loves us, He manifested at the Cross His Justice in His ultimate form, which is Grace. Therefore we are reconciled with Him and we can receive His peace. In the same way, because of God's love in us, we are able to love people. Because we love them, we can seek their good, help them and give them grace if needed as God gave us grace. This brings peace in our relationships.

So peace is not only a spiritual reality that flows from our communion with God in our relationships (as a fruit of the Spirit), but it is also a reality we can bring through decisions we make in manifesting grace and love and righteousness toward one another.

Peace through reconciliation

Reconciliation is an aspect of peace whenever we speak about being a peacemaker or not. Peace can be restored through reconciliation. Jesus brought reconciliation between God and His children, through His own life. This is what gave us access to the peace provided by the adoption of our Father. This is also what we are called to do when we have an opportunity to do so. The Bible exhorts us not to divide brothers, but to "*consider one another in order to stir up love and good works*" (Hebrews 10:24). Encourage reconciliation, or playing an active role in reconciliation between brothers, is a part of being a peacemaker.

Peace through unity

Concerning relationships, the Bible teaches us to seek unity by the binding of peace. It means that seeking unity first is a key to bringing peace. We get more success in bringing peace when our motivation is unity and love.

The way of peace is a fundamental way in God's Kingdom.

To follow Him obviously implies walking with His peace, in what we do and in our relationships with others.

Application

Peace is first an inner wellness and inner happiness that comes from our communion with God. This peace we receive as a gift is supposed to flow in our relationships with others. Our communion with the Holy Spirit empowers us to bring peace around us and to be peacemakers. Peace is always correlated with love, rest, unity, righteousness and grace.

Activation

1- Take a moment to consider peace in your life. Does peace continually dwell in you? Or are there circumstances when you easily lose your peace?

2- Identify these circumstances. Repent for fear, anxiety,

insecurity, anger, panic, stress or anything you identify as an obstacle for peace in those circumstances.

3- Ask God to replace those obstacles with His peace. And take time to receive it.

4- Now, think about a relational situation you are involved in, where the binding of peace has been broken.

5- Ask God to show you how you can participate in restoring peace in the situation.

6- Pray for the people involved in the situation and bless them. Ask God for His eyes to see the situation and the people as He sees them.

7- You can do that each time peace is challenged in a situation you are involved in. And be abundantly blessed in your search for peace. May your peace be multiplied!

6 WAY OF WISDOM

Job 33:33 *"If not, listen to me; hold your peace and I will teach you wisdom."*

God is a God of wisdom. By His wisdom, He created the heavens and the earth. His wisdom is never separated from Him. Everything He does, He does it with His wisdom. As His children, we are called to walk in wisdom as well. Wisdom is one of the ways of the kingdom of God. To walk in the wisdom of God is a part of our calling.

God's wisdom

James 3:13-17 *"Who is wise and understanding among*

you? Let him show by good conduct that his works are done in the meekness of wisdom. But if you have bitter envy and self-seeking in your hearts, do not boast and lie against the truth. This wisdom does not descent from above, but is earthly, sensual, demonic. For where envy and self-seeking exist, confusion and every evil thing are there. But the wisdom that is from above, is first pure, then peacable, gentle, willing to yield, full of mercy and good fruits, without partiality and without hypocrisy."

Proverbs 14:12 *"There is a way that seems right to a man, but its end is the way of death."*

God's ways are not our ways. Human wisdom has nothing to do with God's wisdom. This is why it is vital to seek His council. The Bible says that human wisdom is evil. Human wisdom is opposite from the knowledge of God. It seeks its own thinking, its own human solutions, and its root is sin and evil. Human wisdom leads to confusion and error. It can also lead to destruction, as it does not bring God's will and purpose, which are always life, prosperity, and peace. Wisdom without God is obviously confusion as it proclaims things that are not founded in the truth, who is God.

God's wisdom is correlated with peace, righteousness, grace, truth, holiness, love and kindness. It is obviously

157

associated with all these other ways, as God can never separate Himself from all His attributes. All of them work together and are interacting with one another. God's wisdom then is peaceful, loving, righteous, gracious, holy, and true.

The wisdom of God is perfection. The works of God's wisdom are perfect. In creating things, or doing things, God's wisdom operates in an excellence of knowledge and perfection. In God's wisdom, there is the notion of knowledge. God is omniscient. His wisdom is all together full of knowledge, power, science, and beauty. God never forgets beauty. He is The Creator, The Artist, and everything He does is also beautiful. Beauty is included in His wisdom. *"He has made everything beautiful in its time."* (Ecclesiastes 3:11).

When God does something, all these aspects are measured, perfectly arranged and distributed. God's works last for the duration He has planned them to last. Heaven and Earth are planned to last until the end of this world, and then they will end to make room for a whole new earth and new heavens. Things that are destined to last, last; and things that He has planned just for a while, last for only the period they were meant to last. Seasons, day and night, and seasons in our lives that He orchestrate are all in His hands and timing. God considers all aspects before doing something. There is nothing like His wisdom.

Romans 11:33 *"Oh the depth of the riches both of the wisdom and knowledge of God! How unsearchable are His judgments and His ways past finding out!"*

God's wisdom is powerful. Nothing can come against what He has established and declared. His wisdom is sure and irreversible.

What is wisdom

Wisdom generally means understanding and anticipating the consequences of our actions and words before we act or speak. Biblically, wisdom means having the knowledge and understanding of discerning the right course of action, and having the courage to follow it. It has to do with knowledge, understanding, discernment, and obedience to God to follow His will. It has to do with being enlightened by the Spirit of God to understand situations and to know how to act accordingly.

Wisdom in the Bible generally represents following God and doing His will.

Deuteronomy 4:5-6 *"Surely I have taught you statutes and judgements just as the Lord my God commanded me, that* *you should act according to them in the land which you go to possess. Therefore be careful to observe them, for this is your wisdom and your understanding in the sights of the peoples who will hear all these statutes, and say "surely this great nation is a wise and understanding people."*

He who is wise, according to the Bible, seeks God and follows His Word and His ways. To be wise according to the Scriptures is to seek God's council through the communion with Him and His word and following His ways. The notion of knowledge included in the term "wisdom" always means "to know God and His ways." It has nothing to do with worldly knowledge.

As God is the only true wisdom, we can only be wise in knowing Him and following His will revealed in the Word and through the communion with Him. True wisdom is to seek Him, to meditate on His precepts and to do His will.

At one level, wisdom in the Bible also means "the ability" in some areas like arts or manual works; artisans like weavers, architects, or goldsmiths were considered wise in their skills.

At a second level, wisdom represents a safe way of conduct that is socially, morally and spiritually upright. This is mainly the meaning of wisdom in the book of Proverbs.

Wisdom in the Bible also represents the ability to deal with life and its problems in the right way. Salomon is associated with this idea of "understanding" life and pronouncing the right judgments. He was also known for His wisdom, in the sense of intelligence, knowledge, the way He ruled over the land, and his righteousness.

But these definitions all include the idea of being empowered by God in wisdom. Wisdom can concern different areas, but it is always an ability that comes from the God of wisdom.

The general biblical idea about wisdom is seeking God and following Him and His ways. To act according to His word with the discernment of His Spirit. Intelligence in the Bible always means to seek and to know God.

The idea of seeking Him and His council, following Him and His ways, is fundamental in the notion of wisdom.

Job 28:28 *"And to man, He said: the fear of The Lord, that is wisdom, and to depart from evil, is understanding."*

To fear God means to walk according to His will; it means not only being aware of living before Him but also submitting our actions to His council and following His leading. It is obedience. This is what was requested from the people of Israel each time they had an important decision to make, like entering in war against a nation, as they were taking possession of their promised land. Saul failed to do this in the beginning of his kingship when he didn't wait the assigned time given by God to start a battle, and this is what caused him to lose the crown of Israel.

The fear of the Lord mentioned in the Old Testament still represents the desire to do God's will, to seek Him and follow Him. This is wisdom.

Called to walk in wisdom

Following the way of wisdom is a part of following God and walking in His ways. We are called to manifest His wisdom, as we are supposed to seek His will, to hear His voice, and to meditate on His word. Wisdom, like the other ways of God, flows from our relationship with God, from the meditation of His Word and the communion with His Spirit. But we can also grow in wisdom through the experience of faith and righteousness as well as through knowledge, reflection, and developing our gifts.

Meditate on the word

If we want to walk in wisdom, we need to know God's Word. Only His word teaches us His ways and makes us understand His heart and His mindset. Knowing His word is the beginning of knowing Him. We continually grow in the knowledge of Him, in not only reading, but meditating on the Bible. The meditation of the Word generates wisdom. As we are reading, expecting God to speak to us, He is faithful to speak to us through the Scriptures, and gives us the daily spiritual bread that we need. But as we are meditating on them, something deep is being built and edified in us; this is the knowledge of Him and wisdom.

Joshua 1:8 "*This book of the Law shall not depart from your mouth, but you shall meditate in it day and night, that you may observe to do according to all that is written in it. For then, you will make your way prosperous, and you will have good success.*"

The meditation of the Word helps us walk in His ways and leads us to success. The result of wisdom is prosperity and success.

All levels of the Scriptures contribute to increasing our wisdom as we meditate on them. The practical level, historical level, scientific level, spiritual and even poetic level are all good to make us grow in different aspects of wisdom.

The meditation of the Word helps us know God, His heart, His ways, and it teaches us how to walk in His ways. It builds wisdom in us.

Communion with The Spirit of God

The Spirit of God is a spirit of council. The Holy Spirit is called several times "*Spirit of Council*" and "*Spirit of wisdom*" in the Bible. God is Himself the wisdom, and our wisdom comes from Him. It is in the communion with His Spirit, the Spirit of council, that we can know and grow in wisdom as well.

Walk in the Spirit

God's wisdom consists of walking by the Spirit, and not by the flesh. The flesh will always fight against the Spirit, and our focus must be to surrender to the Holy Spirit in us in every circumstance, to manifest His wisdom and His nature. The communion with the Holy Spirit will always cause us to see situations as He sees them, and will show us how to conduct ourselves accordingly. The walk in the Spirit is obedience to what He shows us, just like Jesus only does what He sees the Father do, and like the Holy Spirit speaks to us the words that He hears from the Father. Jesus promised us that the Holy Spirit would teach us what to say and what to do in all situations as we need it. Our wisdom consists in the obedience of what He shows us to do or to speak.

Wisdom then cancels the desires of the flesh, in being submitted to the Holy Spirit.

Follow God's ways

We have seen how wisdom is correlated with all the other ways of God. Wisdom is actually following God's will and ways, after we understand how He wants us to walk. This is obedience to His ways and His Spirit. Therefore, wisdom is not only knowledge but obedience, action and surrendering to Him. Trust and rest are a part of wisdom, as well as the other ways of God mentioned previously: peace, righteousness, grace, truth, holiness, love and kindness. Because it is showing Him that we rely on Him, and it is letting Him do His part, which is much better than ours.

Following God's ways is wisdom. It is choosing to follow what brings joy to God and what produces life, prosperity and peace in us and around us.

Follow God's principles

A part of wisdom is understanding and following God's principles. Many principles of life and wisdom are given in the Bible to instruct us, to give us examples on how to conduct our lives. The Proverbs are an excellent book to meditate on what wisdom is. It gives many principles of wisdom that are a key for success in life. We can summarize them as follows:

   – Trust God with all your heart, and don't rest on your

own thinking

- don't be lazy

- be humble

- don't lie

- depart from iniquity and do what is righteous

- keep the Word

- don't speak too much

- be righteous

- don't despise your neighbor

- love

- seek council of wisdom

- give

- accept the correction-reprehension from God, and from the wise

- keep your heart with all diligence

- walk in truth

- don't worry

- work for peace

166

- be faithful

- speak blessings and watch your mouth

- hang out with godly people

- correct your children

- use self-control

- bless your parents

These principles are only examples of how to walk in wisdom. They give us an idea of the various wisdoms of God. There are many more principles and rules in the Bible that pertain to wisdom, and it is more important to understand and follow the Spirit of these principles than to strictly observe them like rules. Moreover, some of them refer more to our works and righteousness, others refer to the fruits of the Spirit. It is interesting to notice that in those principles given in the Book of Proverbs, which is known as the book of wisdom (Proverbs 1:1-5), we find a summarization of all the commandments of the Law.

Letting the Holy Spirit rule in us is our best way to walk in wisdom. Most principles of wisdom are actually fulfilled in letting Him rule in us and in walking with Him. When the Bible gives us principles such as letting our words be few, we can fulfill them in letting the Holy Spirit rule in us (which includes self-control) and only speaking what He wants to speak. Some other principles need to be followed by simple obedience, like not often entering the house of our neighbor.

Seek Knowledge

We know that earthly wisdom has nothing to do with true wisdom, the one that comes from knowing God. But we live in a world in which we have to respect the rules and walk wisely. A part of walking in wisdom is seeking knowledge in order to understand the world in which we live, and also being able to make decisions to adjust our actions accordingly.

Scientific, historical, economic, political and geographical knowledge will always help us to make the right decisions, to better know how to walk in righteousness and wisdom in the world in which we live. It will always make us realize how this world needs to be reconciled with God through Jesus and compel us to do something about it at our level.

We are the Light of the world, and we are supposed to help people around us understand the true meaning of life in the light of the Gospel. Whatever is our area of influence in life, we are called to bring God's Light in this area. Knowledge then is a key to confronting the lies of the enemy (like in history, for example) or unrighteousness with the Truth.

Knowledge then is a part of wisdom as well.

Intelligence, Reflection and Common sense

Nehemiah 5:7 "*After serious thought, I rebuked the nobles and rulers, and said to them 'each of you is exacting usuring from his brother.' So I called a great assembly against them. And I said to them 'according to our ability we have redeemed our Jewish brethren who were sold to the nations. Now indeed, will you even sell your brethren? Or should they be sold to us?' Then, they were silent and found nothing to say. Then I said 'what you are doing is not good. Should you not walk in the fear of The Lord because of the reproach of the nations, our ennemies? I also with my brethren and my servants am lending them money and grain. Please let us stop this usury. Restore now to them, even this day, their lands, their vineyards, their olive groves, and their houses, also a hundredth of the money and the grain, the new wine and the oil, that you have charged them.' So they said 'we will restore it and will require nothing from them; we will do as you say.'"*

In this passage, we see Nehemiah establishing righteousness between the Hebrews, "**after serious thought**". This expression shows that Nehemiah didn't have to consult God or some prophets to know what to do. He deeply considered and thought about the situation, according to *"the fear of The Lord"*. His wisdom consisted in using reflection, according to the Word of God. His wisdom was acknowledged by all the people who obeyed what he suggested.

God has given us an ability for reflection, for intellectual activity, and He expects us to use it. To seek God for directions and leading doesn't exclude us from walking in maturity and using our own reflection. Sometimes, God prefers us to walk in intelligence and trusts us in our judgments and decisions. As we grow in Him, He trusts us in our reflection and decisions because He knows in advance we have been trained in His word and know what pleases Him. He doesn't expect us to ask Him about any small decision we have to make. He trusts us to walk according to His word, in the balance of common sense, reflection and maturity.

When Abraham's blessing expanded so that both he and Lot couldn't stay in the same land, he simply asked Lot to choose what part of the land he wanted. He didn't consult God for this. This was wisdom to let Lot choose his part first, to prevent any further eventual contest. We see here how wisdom includes love, kindness, peace and faith that God would bless Abraham as He promised him.

God expects us to walk in maturity, using common sense, reflection and intelligence. This is a part of wisdom – to use the ability to think, discern and ponder things that God has given us. As long as our soul is fed with the word of God and our will is to align with His will in seeking Him, reflection is helpful and safe.

An outstanding conduct

We find many examples of characters who were walking in wisdom in the Bible. One of them is Abigail, Nabab's wife. In Samuel 25:3 it is said that she was a woman "*of good understanding*". Her conduct and words toward David saved her life and the lives of all her house and servants. David blessed and praised her with these words, "*Blessed is your advice.*"

She came with abundant provisions for David and his people as they were fleeing from Saul, after her husband refused to help him. She also gave David the good advice not to avenge himself with his own hands, to let God do His justice and for this not to be an obstacle to his peace when he will become king. She also spoke words of encouragement to him, acknowledging that he will certainly become king of Israel, according to God's words.

In what she did and spoke to David, we can see several

aspects of wisdom – a driven and appropriate action at the right time, humility, courage, righteousness and goodness, generosity, peace, and the ability to speak words of wisdom and intelligence. We clearly see that these words she spoke were coming from the Spirit of God.

Through this example, we can see how wisdom includes several aspects that work together. These are actually the ways and character of God manifested, with the leading of His Spirit.

Develop Gifts and Creativity

We have seen that abilities and gifts are considered as "wisdom" in the Bible. The men who were chosen to build the tabernacle according to the model Moses had received from God were considered wise because of their abilities and gifts. The musicians and singers who were leading worship in the Old Testament were considered "intelligent" because of their gifts. They were all operating in the Spirit of excellence that glorifies God.

Gifts and abilities all come from God and are a part of His ability. He has created the heavens and the earth by His wisdom, and all that we receive from Him is a part of His wisdom.

Therefore, developing the gifts and abilities He has

deposited in our lives is also wisdom. We have received those gifts to partake in the advancement of His Kingdom, and we participate in His wisdom if we seek to develop what He has given us to achieve His purpose. We glorify God when we walk fully into the destiny He has planned for us, operating in the gifts He gave us, developing them in the Spirit of excellence.

Power

God created the heavens and the earth by His wisdom. His wisdom is a power. It is not only an abstract concept but also a power that accomplishes things. We have received the Spirit of God who contains His wisdom, and therefore we can walk in this power of creativity and accomplishment. If wisdom is also a power, then we are supposed to walk and grow in that power continually. This power can be manifested in many ways: in healings and miracles, wonders, creativity, etc.

Experience

Job 12:12 *"Wisdom is with aged men, and with length of days, understanding."*

It is obvious that wisdom increases with experience and spiritual maturity. Experience in the faith provides maturity which produces wisdom. Wisdom is walking in the ways of

173

God all together; therefore, we can grow in wisdom by growing in each of the ways of God.

The more we learn how to walk in all the ways of God, the more we grow in wisdom.

Wisdom, a successful walk in all the ways of God

James 3:17 *"But the wisdom that is from above is first pure, then peacable, gentle, willing to yield, full of mercy and good fruits, without partiality, and without hypocrisy."*

Analyzing all the characteristics of wisdom mentioned in the Bible, we notice that biblical wisdom actually mainly represents walking in all the ways of God (holiness, peace, love, righteousness, truth, faith) to manifest the fruits of the Spirit and to walk in the Spirit.

To practice righteousness, in love, peace, holiness and truth, to walk with the discernment of the Holy Spirit, and to manifest the fruits of the Spirit is actually wisdom. The discernment of the Holy Spirit teaches us what to say or what to do in each situation, every time we need it. We don't always know what our words or actions will produce in others' lives, even using reflection and sometimes experience. This is why we need the help of the Holy Spirit to show us how to behave in each situation. Having the right attitude, making the right decision, speaking the right words, adopting the right strategy – all of this can be achieved with the help of the Holy Spirit, who is the Spirit of wisdom.

What does it mean that wisdom involves walking in all the ways of God? If we take the example of love, we must understand that wisdom seeks love. Its purpose and motivation is love. We must remember that love is supposed to be the source of all that we do. Just as the sense of righteousness is love, the sense of wisdom is love. This is what makes it completely opposite to an earthly or carnal wisdom. Our actions, plans, and conversations must be driven by love, which always releases the approval and the help of the Spirit of God. It provides the best ground for wisdom. Solomon received an incomparable wisdom because He asked God to help him lead the people. His prayer was a prayer of love for the people. His heart was to provide for the people a safe, peaceful and righteous place to live.

Then, as all the other ways of God are correlated with love, wisdom contains all of them. There is no true wisdom without love, peace, truth, righteousness, faith, and holiness. Faith is necessary in wisdom, first because our wisdom comes from God and also because as God shows us what to do or what to say, we must believe that the results of obeying Him will be successful.

We have seen with the example of Abigail how wisdom actually includes all the ways of God together, with the leading of the Holy Spirit. It represents the right and driven action that shows understanding of the situation, and it is a response of excellence in this situation.

To walk in all the ways of God, to follow Him, and to obey His Holy Spirit is wisdom.

Wisdom brings success

Proverbs 3:13-18 *"Happy is the man who finds wisdom, and the man who gains understanding; for her proceeds are better than the profits of silver, and her gain than fine gold. She is more precious than rubies, and all the things you may desire cannot compare with her. Length of days is in her right hands, in her left hand riches and honor. Her ways are ways of pleasantness, and all her paths are peace. She is a tree of life for those who take hold of her, and happy are all who retain her."*

1 Samuel 18:14 *"And David behaved wisely in all his ways, and The Lord was with him."*

Ecclesiastes 10:10 *"If the ax is dull, and one does not* *sharpen the edge, then he must use more strength; but wisdom brings success."*

As wisdom anticipates the results and fruits of its plans, and does it with the knowledge of God that cannot fail, wisdom then leads inevitably to success. The Spirit of wisdom is a Spirit of life, multiplication, triumph and victory. Following Him leads us to prosperity and abundant life. Whatever area in which we walk in wisdom, we will see this area of our lives prosper. Whether it is an ability or gift that we develop with the Holy Spirit or simply an area in which we walk in wisdom, it will always be fruitful and lead us to success.

God's ways are prosperous; therefore, if we practice them all together, it will inevitably lead us to success in all that we do. It is said that the Word of God never returns without any effect; therefore, if we practice it with the Holy Spirit, it will always produce good fruit.

Wisdom, a key for righteousness

1 Kings 3:28 *"And all Israel heard of the judgment which the king had rendered; and they feared the king for they saw that the wisdom of God was in Him to administer justice."*

James 3:13 *"Who is wise and understanding among you?*

177

Let him show by good conduct that his works are done in the meekness of wisdom."

Righteousness and wisdom work together, as we saw that all the ways of God work together. It is obvious that in wisdom there is an understanding and intelligence that helps walk in righteousness. Intelligence in the Bible always means "understanding of the Word and the ways of God" and "knowing God". Solomon was known for his wisdom because he was actually giving right judgments that were directly inspired by the Spirit of God. He had a discernment that could only come from God.

Wisdom is a key for righteousness, but we also grow in wisdom with the experience and practice of righteousness.

Jesus is our wisdom

1 Corinthians 1:30 *"But of Him you are in Christ Jesus, who became for us wisdom from God, and righteousness, and sanctification, and redemption."*

The Bible invites us to ask for God's wisdom if we lack wisdom. He answers our prayers and gives us wisdom when we need it. Jesus was made wisdom for us. He lives in us through the Holy Spirit, and He says that His sheep hear His voice. We can receive His thought and understand

His will on each situation, as long as we remain in a true communion with Him. God loves to collaborate with us. He loves to interact with us, to teach and show us things.

Jesus is not only the one who gives us wisdom, but He is our wisdom. This means that God considers us wise from the moment we receive Him as Savior and Lord. He knows He is able to accomplish anything for us. Therefore, to receive Him as the Son of God who saves is for Him the wisest decision we can make. God knows we need Him and that our human understanding and ways are limited. This is why He also considers us wise when we come to Him, because He knows we receive then His ability to walk in wisdom.

Jesus is our wisdom, which also means that when situations are beyond us, He is able to work things out for us, without our own intervention. When we are needy or feel unqualified, He is the one who takes our defense and works for us.

Application

We are called to walk in God's wisdom. This is a high calling as it represents the ability to follow the totality of God's ways. Manifesting God's wisdom is a mark of being kings and queens of God. Like David and Solomon were able to manifest God's wisdom, how much more are we supposed to walk in God's wisdom, we who have received Jesus who has fully reconciled us with our heavenly Father, we who have received the Holy Spirit, and we who have a revelation of the whole Scriptures (Old and New Testament).

God's wisdom seeks love, peace, and righteousness. It operates in purity, kindness, grace, humility and all the good fruits of the Spirit (James 3:17). It consists of a conduct that manifests all the ways of God, as well as the fruits of the Spirit.

It consists of a conduct, an attitude, a plan, actions, or/and words that reflect the intelligence, the excellence, and mercy of God.

Activation

1- Think about a situation in which you feel you have not walked in God's wisdom.

2- Identify the points or the reasons why you didn't walk in God's wisdom.

3- Ask God to strengthen you in these areas.

4- Think now about a current situation in which you need wisdom.

5- Identify the key ways of God you would need to follow to walk in wisdom in this situation.

6- Ask God to help you walk in these ways, and ask Him to give you a clear insight of what you should do.

7- Observe the fruits of your decision, and ask God for wisdom each time you need it.

7 WAY OF FAITH

Our Christian walk is supposed to be the fruit of a true faith, a clear and total conviction that produces actions according to it that are founded on the Bible. Faith in Jesus as God, our only Savior and Lord, who came to give us access to the Father and to eternal abundant life is fundamental. It is our point of departure for our Christian walk, but is also a lifestyle. Any of our actions must be led by faith. We are supposed to live all our lives by faith.

Faith is a way we are called to walk in during all our lives, and not in our conversion only.

About faith

Ephesians 2:8 *"For by grace you have been saved through faith, and that not of yourselves; it is the gift of God, not of works, lest anyone should boast."*

Romans 10:10 *"For with the heart, one believes unto righteousness, and with the mouth confession is made unto salvation."*

Faith is not believing that God exists but is truly believing what He says and obeying Him. Faith is founded in our love for God. He first loved us, and once we realize His love for us, which is when faith begins, our faith grows as our love for Him grows. Faith without love is vain and not fruitful. (1 Corinthians 13:2).

Faith involves all areas of our lives: salvation, spirit, soul, body (God saves us, provides for us and heals us), our works, our ways, our decisions and actions. It is literally a lifestyle, founding everything we do on faith. Faith includes trust, patience, obedience to God, and perseverance. It is a decision that leads to actions and choices that demonstrate our trust in God. It is not a passive waiting. In all areas of our lives, we are supposed to live in faith.

Faith is a gift from God. Only God can open our eyes to the Truth, as we don't see the spiritual realm with our human eyes. Each Christian received this gift of faith from God, as it is said that no one can come to the Light unless the Father has drawn them. But once we receive faith, we enter in a covenant and a communion with Him that enables us to collaborate with Him in all these areas. For example, when it comes to jobs, we know He provides for us, but we have to do our part in seeking and finding the job.

Faith then is an active collaboration with God in all areas of our lives, showing that we trust Him with what He leads us to, receiving what He gives us and doing what He wants with it.

Called to walk by faith

Habakkuk 2:4 *"Behold the proud, his soul is not upright in him; but the just shall live by his faith."*

2 Corinthians 5:7 *"For we walk by faith, not by sight."*

Without faith, it is impossible to please God. Faith in Him is all that we have to present to God. Even though it is a gift given by God, He expects us to walk in it. To activate it, to walk in it, and to keep it.

In Luke 1:20, when Zacharias, John the Baptist's father, was told by the angel Gabriel the good news that he would birth a son whom God will use to prepare His people to receive Christ, he became mute for a while because he didn't immediately believe the word that was spoken to him. God doesn't like incredulity. Incredulity is like an offense to Him. But He always remunerates faith.

For all of us, there are areas in which we have great faith, and some others in which our faith needs to grow. This is because of our tendency to believe that some subjects are more difficult for God to resolve. And our scale in this is even completely subjective, correlated to the way we perceive things and not based on an objective reality. The reality, though, is that God can do everything. For Him there are not things that are more difficult to accomplish than others. It is stunning how we can have big faith for big things and small faith for little things sometimes.

The truth is all things are possible for God. They are not big things or small things for God. He is the Big God for everything.

Be like a child

Jesus gave us a key to walk in faith in becoming like a child. In Luke 18:17, He declares that anyone who doesn't receive the Kingdom of God like a child won't enter it. There is a power in believing like a child. It opens wide the gates of

Heaven. All the sick who were hoping to touch Jesus while He was ministering on earth were healed, simply because of their faith like a child. Jesus said to several of them, "Your faith healed you."

One day, I realized that in many prophetic experiences where I was with God, I was appearing as a little girl. I then asked God why I was appearing like that, and not as an adult. I was thinking about the reality that as His sons and daughters we are in His Kingdom princes and princesses, kings and queens. When I asked Him why I was seeing me like a little girl in these visions, God immediately answered to me, *"Because nobody can enter my Kingdom unless he becomes like a child."*

The prayers of children are always very interesting; they are very simple, straight, and certain that God can do all things.

To believe like a child is a key to walk in faith. It is receiving His promises without any doubt or any question on how He will operate the fulfillment. To simply be sure that what He said, He will do.

How can we believe like a child when we are not children? If God tells us to believe like children, it is because we have the ability to do so. Faith is a gift, and we have to receive the same gift of faith as children. The gift of faith given to children is the same that was given to us. The only difference between us and children is the experience of life. Bad experiences in life before knowing God, wrong decisions we made, failures, sin – all of these can be an obstacle to faith. Therefore, a lack of faith in some areas is often correlated with sin. For example, many times fear is an obstacle to faith. That kind of sin can sometimes predominate and spoil our faith or make it unavailable.

The good news is that Jesus has defeated all powers of darkness, and that we are no longer condemned to live with them. As soon as we realize there is something that can prevent our faith from being what it should be, we can declare ourselves free in the name of Jesus. We can identify those things that spoil the faith we have received as a gift, and then remove them.

The Gospel is simple. Simple and powerful. Jesus has overcome all things for us. He has finished all things. We simply have to receive it as a wonderful gift to us.

In heaven, people don't have any issue with faith. They continually live in the middle of the Glory of God, can contemplate His face as much as they want, can see Him and hear Him continually. In Eden, in the beginning of the Creation, men had no issue of faith either because they were close to God and sin had not entered in their heart yet. We are supposed to live in the same standard of faith as all those in heaven, and those who have been before us, in the beginning of the world because we are children of God. Today, if our faith is not what it should be, it is because of sin. Therefore, we must identify what the obstacles of our faith are in our lives and remove them.

We can live the same standard of faith as all our brothers and sisters in heaven, since we have entered the kingdom of God and already received the promise of eternal life by the faith in Jesus. Eternal and abundant life has started for us since we accepted Jesus as Lord and Savior, and since we have received the Holy Spirit who connects us to Him. We can live in the same standard of faith as all the powerful men and women of faith in history if we remove the stones of our hearts. Jesus said, *"Blessed are the pure in heart, for they shall see God."* (Matthew 5:8). A pure heart seeks after God, wants to please Him, and believes what He says.

Demonstrate faith by our actions

2 Corinthians 4:13 *"And since we have the same spirit of faith, according to what is written, 'I believed and therefore, I spoke,' we also believe and therefore speak."*

James 2:14-17 *"What does it profit my brethren, if someone* *says he has faith but does not have works? Can faith save him? If a brother or sister is naked and destitute of daily food, and one of you say to them: 'Depart in peace, be warmed and filled,' and you do not give them the things which are needed for the body, what does it profit? Thus also faith by itself, if it does not have works, is dead."*

To walk in faith implies works, acts, and actions. Faith without works is dead. When we think about this verse, we generally think about the kind of works like helping the poor and manifesting righteousness to those who are needy. This is a part of what the church is supposed to do, but we forget that faith implies all kinds of actions and decisions in our daily life that are directly connected to what we believe. The simple act of reading the Bible daily comes from the faith that it is the spiritual food we need for life, and that God is going to speak to us through our daily reading.

Faith must determine our actions. Our works and actions demonstrate what we believe.

Faith often implies acts that we do to show God we count on Him to do His part in situations. If we have a conviction for something, we can be led to act as if what we believe is coming to pass. These are acts of faith. These are necessary to collaborate with God in what He wants to do.

189

We show Him we understand what He wants to do, and that we are with Him in what He has planned. Acts of faith are an active participation with the Holy Spirit, in the direction of what God wants to operate, and we cannot see them by sight yet. By them, we demonstrate an active walk on earth, having our eyes fixed on the Sovereign God and obeying what He says. They prepare the way for the fulfillment of the promises of God and what He wants to accomplish. Rahab, the woman of Jericho who helped the two Hebrew spies, did an act of faith in hiding them in her house. She believed God would give Jericho to the Hebrews, and then she risked her life to hide them by faith. Her act of faith saved her and all her family.

Our attitude toward bad circumstances also defines our faith. Thankfulness, worship, peace, and joy are reflections of our faith during trial seasons. Our faith can be measured by our ability to remain in peace, in joy, and in a thankful attitude toward The Lord in seasons of trials. This is how we are supposed to walk. The Bible invites us to rejoice in all circumstances, for God walks before us, in all things, and because He reigns over our lives to make all things work together for our good, as long as we follow Him.

Live by true faith

We can walk in all the other ways of God because of faith. We can love others because we know we are loved by God. We can live in holiness because by faith we receive His holiness. We can live in righteousness because we receive His righteousness by faith, etc.

Faith always comes first in the Kingdom of God if we want to walk in all the other ways of God. We cannot enter the kingdom of God without faith, and we cannot do anything without faith.

As God can do all things, we can do all things with Him, by faith.

Philippians 4:13 *"I can do all things through Christ who strengthens me."*

The Bible says that if we have faith, at least just a little bit of faith, we can move mountains. It is interesting to think that Jesus said that only a little faith can operate big things like moving mountains. He gave this example to say that we can do everything by faith. The example of moving mountains can be understood in the literal sense as well as in the figurative sense. We can do all things if only we have a little bit of faith. This statement is powerful because it reveals the power of true faith. When Jesus declared this, He was speaking to His disciples who were following Him and were operating miracles of healings. They had faith, and were manifesting some signs of faith, but according to Jesus, their faith was not complete.

Matthew 17:20 *"So Jesus said to them, 'because of your unbelief, for assuredly, I say to you, if you have faith as a mustard seed, you will say to this mountain: "move from here to there", and it will move ; and nothing will be impossible for you.'"*

He actually considered their faith as unbelief because it was not whole. Their faith was not total; it was spoiled by doubt. For God, faith spoiled by doubts is unbelief. True faith is faith without any doubt. It is the faith that empowers us to walk on water and to move mountains. True faith is whole, sure and constant. God delights Himself in meeting that kind of faith.

We are called to walk in true faith, a faith that doesn't hesitate. This is the only faith by which all things are possible to us.

How can we boost our faith?

There are factors that have the ability to increase our faith.

Intimacy with God

Intimacy with God is the first element that increases our

faith. From our relationship with God, our faith can be strengthened and become deeper. When we spend time with Him, letting Him speak and touch us, transform and comfort us, we experience the tangible action of His presence on us. This experience encourages our faith and reminds us of the reality of the God we love. It places our faith in the dimension of the reality of God. There is no faith booster like this one. Intimacy with the Lord makes us love Him more and more. Once we taste the wonder of being in His presence, we want to reiterate the experience as often as we can. He becomes then the delight of our life. The more we spend quality time with Him, the more we are in love with Him, and the less we are attracted to this world. To be in love with Jesus increases our faith, because when we love, we believe.

1 Corinthians 13:7 *"Love believes all things."*

Love produces and increases faith. Also, when we are no longer attracted to this world and its distractions, our eyes and our hearts can be focused on what pleases God and on what He wants. We can then better walk in faith.

Meditation of the Word of God

Romans 10:17 *"So then, faith comes by hearing, and hearing by the word of God."*

Mediation on the word of God is an essential faith builder. If we know that faith comes from our contact with the Word of God, then setting quality time apart to hear God through His Word helps us build our faith. To voluntarily spend some time in the meditation of the Bible on specific topics will also make our faith grow on these topics.

Obedience

Another faith booster is obedience. Obedience to God will always produce good fruits. Obeying Him and following Him, in spite of what the circumstances may look like, is an act of faith. God always remunerates obedience. This experience of always seeing our obedience being recompensed inevitably strengthens our faith.

Suffering

Suffering helps to deepen our faith. In the suffering, God operates many healings in us and deepens our longing for Him. Suffering is a well that God digs for us in order to fill it afterwards with His abundant life and joy. The deeper the well is, the more blessings that will come out of it. Our present suffering is a future source of joy and provision of life for others.

Here we are discussing the suffering allowed by God to perfect us and to prepare us for what He has called us to be and to do. It excludes all other kinds of suffering: suffering as a result of disobedience to God, or sin, or the works of the flesh, etc.

There are seasons of suffering that God allows in our lives to reinforce our communion with Him, to deepen our faith, purify us, heal us, and empower us for what He has called us to. They may last for a short time or long time, but they always have a purpose that God has fully measured. These seasons of suffering are necessary for our growth and to mature our faith. They are always followed with great fulfillments and blessings. The greatest example of those seasons in life in the Bible is Job. Remember how Job was abundantly blessed after the season of suffering he endured. It is said that he was blessed with double that he had in the beginning. Faith then will always get deeper once we realize how much God has done through these seasons of trials, and how much greater the benefits of it are in comparison to the suffering.

Experience

Experience always confirms the sovereignty of God, His faithfulness and goodness. Whatever circumstances we may go through, sooner or later, as children of God, we always experience that all things works together for our good. We are more than conquerors in Jesus in all things, and the experience of faithfulness of God builds and increases our faith.

Application

Faith sustains all the other ways of God. It is the key that gives us access to the Kingdom of God and enables us to walk in all the other ways of God. Faith is first a gift, but it is meant to grow as we exercise it. The more we walk in faith and trust, the more we experience the faithfulness of God, and the more our faith grows.

Our faith is defined by the actions, acts and works that we do. There is no faith without actions. Our attitude toward circumstances also demonstrates what we believe.

Only true faith gives us access to all accomplishments. Only true faith in the Almighty God makes all things possible for us.

Activation

1-Think about a current situation in which you need a greater measure of faith.

2- Take a moment with God and ask Him to show you what elements spoil your faith in the situation.

3- Ask God to remove those elements and replace them with faith and confidence. Repent if necessary and thank God for His wonderful work at the Cross. If He doesn't show you any elements, simply ask Him to increase your faith.

4- Declare yourself free to live by faith in the situation.

5- Renew it each time your faith is being challenged.

CONCLUSIONS ON GOD'S WAYS

We see that all the ways of God we are called to walk in are a reflection both of who God is and what He loves. We are called to be a reflection of who He is: love, holiness, righteousness, peace, truth, and wisdom. We are called to walk in what He loves: love, faith, holiness, righteousness, peace, truth, and wisdom. We notice that what He loves is actually everything that is good for us. He loves faith because He knows it is our salvation; it is more than good for us. Without faith, we cannot enter into His promises. He loves to see in us love and holiness because He knows this is what unlocks the doors of Heaven in our lives. (Those who are pure at heart shall see God). He loves to see us walk in truth and peace because it is the key for our freedom and happiness. He loves to see righteousness and wisdom in us because He knows it is the key for us for a prosperous life.

He loves us above all. So what He loves is directly bound to what is good for us.

He loves to see us walk in His ways because He knows it is

the key for us for an abundant and prosperous life for eternity.

Following His ways is not a matter of simple obedience; otherwise it would be exactly the same thing as fanaticism or following a religion. But following His ways is a matter of love – not only a matter of us loving Him, but the fact that He loves us. Even the ten commandments that represent the whole law, in spite of the imperative mood, are actually a promise He makes us to be able to walk in this, if we follow Him by heart. Each commandment is a promise that we are able to fulfill it by simply receiving His love. For example, when He commands us, *"You shall not commit adultery,"* or even not to covet, which is also adultery, He indirectly makes us the promise that we will find everything we need to be content with the spouse He gave us. When He commands us not to steal, He indirectly promised us He would provide work for us. His commandments are a way of saying to us, *"You will be able to make it, because I did everything for you to be able to do it."*

Following His ways, therefore, is not only a matter of obedience to Him, but a matter of Love. Not only our love for Him, but first His love for us that empowers us to obey His ways. It is His love for us that is the source of all things and the sense of all things.

1 John 5:3 *"For this is the love of God that we keep His commandments."*

His love for us is our ability to follow His ways. His love for us leads us into the destiny He has planned for us, to be His children and to live the plans and purposes He has for us.

We can follow all His ways, only because HE loves us.

Our love for Him is only a response to HIS love, the source of all things. We aren't expected anything from God, except to simply receive HIS love. And His love empowers us, by faith, to do anything that pleases Him.

The glorious circle

To summarize God's seven ways, and the fact that the love of God is the source of everything in God's kingdom, here is a simple visual presentation.

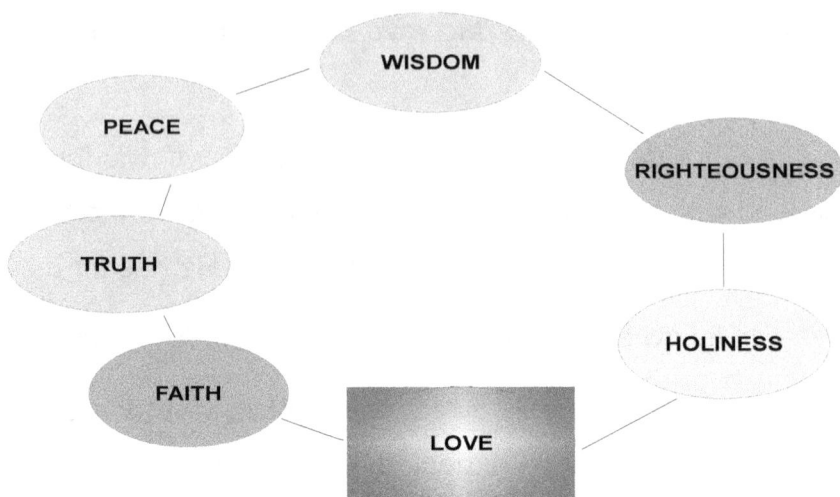

Interactions

We covered that all the ways of God are in correlation with one another.

The main way, which is at the source of any other ways in the Kingdom, is Love. Without love, we cannot truly walk in any other way of God. And without love, anything that we do is vain. Because of love, our faith grows. Because of love, we seek peace, truth and holiness, and we can walk in righteousness and wisdom.

Because of faith, we love and our love grows. We can walk

in holiness and righteousness. We can live in peace, we receive the truth, and we can walk in wisdom.

Holiness interacts with peace, truth, and faith and makes it easier to walk in righteousness and wisdom.

Peace works for love, righteousness, and wisdom. It is a part of holiness and truth and is received by faith.

Truth works for love, holiness, righteousness, and wisdom. It is a part of holiness and is received by faith.

Righteousness works for love, peace, and truth with holiness, wisdom and faith.

Wisdom is a combination of walking in love, holiness, righteousness, peace, truth and faith.

Each way is an important part of who God is, how He walks, and how we are destined to walk in God's Kingdom. Each of them proceeds from who God is and how He operates and represents how He expects us to walk.

It is God's love first that enables and empowers us to walk in His ways. His love manifested in grace, power, and the life of the Holy Spirit in us.

II- HOW TO WALK

IN ALL THE WAYS OF GOD

Proverbs 3:6 *"In all your ways acknowledge Him, and He shall direct your paths."*

To walk with God involves walking in all His ways.

There are many promises in walking in all the ways of God. To acknowledge Him in all our ways actually means to walk in all His ways. The first promise attached to this is that The Lord will always direct us and lead us. He will always make our path sure and make His will known, if we are willing to follow His ways. Many more promises are attached to each way of God when we follow them, like:

About love: when we love, we receive love. This is the promise for the giver, that he will receive. There is also a promise of fullness in love. Only love can provide a true and full contentment.

About holiness: those who are pure will see God. A promise of revelation and intimacy with God is attached to holiness and purity.

In general, walking in all the ways of God, following Him, obeying Him, and loving Him gives us access to all the heavenly and earthly blessings. God made us the promise of an abundant and prosperous life, of His faithfulness and provision for any of our needs.

Ephesians 1:3 *"Blessed be the God and the Father of our Lord Jesus-Christ, who has blessed us with every spiritual blessing in the heavenly places in Christ."*

Matthew 19:29 *"And everyone who has left houses, or brothers or sisters, or father or mother, or wife, or children or lands, for my name's sake, shall receive a hundredfold, and inherit eternal life."*

Keys to successfully follow all the ways of God

Two keys have appeared when analyzing how to walk in

each way of God: the communion with God and the meditation of His word. These same keys are obviously effective in the pursuit of walking in all the ways of God, with three others. We can summarize all of them as follows:

1- Communion with God

We have covered the fact that in order to walk in any of God's ways, we need to be and remain in communion with Him. This is the first main key to follow all His ways as well. The communion with The Lord is the base of everything in our Christian life. From there we receive His love, His guidance, His restoration and consolation, His encouragement, etc. It is the place where our motivation to please Him grows.

Worship is an important part of our relationship with God. Communion with Him inevitably compels us to worship Him. His transforming presence compels us into thankfulness and worship. Worship then prepares us to walk in all His ways; it moves us off-center from ourselves and makes us focus on the One who reigns. It makes us focus on His greatness and His Sovereignty, which encourages our faith.

2- Meditation on the Word of God

2 Timothy 3:16 "*All scripture is given by inspiration of God, and is profitable for doctrine, for reproof, for correction, for* *instruction in righteousness, that the man of God may be complete, thoroughly equipped for every good work."*

Our meditation on the Bible is a part of our communion with God. The first way for God to speak to us is through His word. The demonstration of His love for His people throughout the whole Bible, the mention of His creation, His acts of power, signs and wonders in all history, makes us know His nature and character and increases our desire to know Him personally. The word instructs us and teaches us about the conduct we are supposed to walk in. It edifies us and builds our wisdom.

3- Grace

To follow God and walk in all His ways is only possible by His grace. We cannot do it by ourselves. He gave us everything for us to be able to walk in His ways. We have received the Holy Spirit who enables us to walk "according to the law of the Spirit of Life". The Holy Spirit in us empowers us to walk according to His nature and grow in the character of God. It is important to understand that we receive everything from God by grace. The sacrifice of Jesus at the Cross is the mercy of God for us that propels us by faith into a position of glory: redeemed, sanctified and justified children of God, seated in the heavenly places with

God.

Any power of darkness has been defeated, and we are no longer under the condemnation of living in sin. We are declared justified, sanctified by the Blood of Jesus. He has won all for us already. He has finished everything. By faith, we can walk in all the glorious ways of God, because of the Grace of God.

Being able to follow God and walk in all His ways is an inheritance we receive as children of God. His inheritance is an abundant and prosperous life, full of the Holy Spirit: the Spirit of Life. And the only way to successfully walk in it is to simply receive it by faith, knowing it is God's grace for us.

The success in walking in all the ways of God resides in this main key: to accept and receive that God Himself has already made the way for us to be successful in walking in all His ways. This is the sure key to be confident that we can make it – to understand, believe and receive that He has actually made it for us.

We are victorious in walking in all the ways of God, knowing that God has already made the way for us for it. We receive it as an inheritance, by faith.

4- Love

God's love for us is our energy. It must be the source of our motivation for everything in the kingdom of God, so in our lives in general. God's love for us is the source of any capacity in our lives. Understanding that we can only walk in His ways because He first loved us is a key to be willing to follow Him and to be successful in living His ways.

1 John 5:3 *"For this is the love of God that we keep His commandments."*

God is the first one to be after our happiness and prosperity. He wants our souls as our lives to be prosperous, and for us to fully live this abundant life He promised us for eternity. And He knows the condition for it is to follow Him and His ways. So He gave everything for us to be able to follow His ways.

His love is the source of everything in the Kingdom, and the foundation of our relationship with God. We follow Him because we love Him. We love Him because we know Him. We know Him, and it makes us love Him more. It is only through this love that we can follow Him and His ways.

Understanding that from His love comes our capacity to walk in each of His ways is important in our walk with Him.

Also, love must be the motivation for us in all that we do. This is the key to be successful in all His ways.

5- The glorious circle

We have seen how all the ways of God are connected to one another. Each progression in one of God's ways leads to positive repercussions in our walk in some others areas. Each victory in one way of God we follow leads to a positive impact in our walk in some other ways of the Kingdom. This is the principle of the glorious circle. Each step, each victory positively impacts other areas of our walk with God. This is the exponential blessing of following Him.

And this is also what **2 Corinthians 3** means when it says, *"But we all...are being transformed into the same image, from glory to glory.."* We are destined to live from glory to glory in the Kingdom of God, as long as we follow Him and seek Him. This verse speaks about us being transformed to the image of God through the communion and relationship with Him, through spending time in His presence.

But it is also true that we are meant to grow from glory to glory, as we follow His ways. Each step in walking in His ways is a step into more of His glory in our lives. Each success in walking in one of His ways opens doors for success in our walk in other ways of God. This is how the glorious circle works.

This must encourage us in our pursuit of God.

Also, it is important to not let us get discouraged by any

failure in some areas while walking with God. Some areas of our lives may take more time to get aligned with the standard of God. It can sometimes take a process and reeducation. One key then is to proclaim the Word and try again until it works! Because it will inevitably work one day, as the Word is True, and God is faithful. In this case, we can strengthen ourselves and be encouraged by the areas in which we are stronger.

We have spoken about the fact that to successfully walk in God's ways is an inheritance. An inheritance is something we receive as a gift, freely. But then we have to walk in this inheritance; we have to steward and manage it and make it prosper.

This is the same with what God has given us. He has freely given us the ability to walk in the high calling of living His ways. But we still have to do our part. We have to walk in it and make this wonderful inheritance prosper.

III- HOW TO KNOW GOD'S WILL

IN ANY SITUATION

To walk in God's ways is a lifestyle. It involves our character, our heart, our motivations, the stewardship of our thoughts and emotions, as well as our conduct and actions.

It is then our way of being and living; it reflects who we are and who we trust.

To follow God's ways involves all the areas of our lives and concerns all our decisions.

Now, we need to understand how following God's ways can define our daily life and our decisions. We need to concretely understand how to know God's will in each situation while following His ways.

Nothing is and will ever be more important than our relationship and communion with the Living God. From this loving relationship comes the glorious destiny we are called to. To seek Him, to listen to Him, to let Him minister to us and love on us is the most essential and precious good we have. From this relationship, we can know what pleases God and what is His will for our lives. He leads us as we ask Him to do so and we let Him do so.

Nothing will ever replace the communion with God, which He is so jealous about. It is the key for our lives and destiny.

That being said, as His sons and daughters, God wants us to walk in maturity and responsibility. He has given us everything to discern how to walk according to His word and His will. As long as we follow Him and remain in Him in a deep and true communion with Him, He will always lead us.

Following His ways actually means to follow Him. We have seen that in order to walk in any of the ways of God, the communion with Him is essential. To walk in His ways actually involves following Him. Walking in His ways guarantees that we please Him and offers us a sure path in any situation. It provides clarity in what we are supposed to do in each situation.

In other words, being aware of God's ways and following them in oneness with God's Spirit guarantees us to be in God's will in every situation.

In this chapter, we just want to bring several more keys that can help us to know God's will for every situation, knowing that nothing will ever replace the communion with God and the meditation of His word.

Several main tools can help us to peacefully discern what God's will is for every situation.

1- Ask God to lead you

The first thing we need to do when needing to discern God's will in a situation is simply to ask Him to lead us in what we should do.

This may seem so simple, but many times most Christians forget to ask God to lead them when they have to make important decisions.

God generally trusts us to steward our daily lives and the daily decisions we have to make, according to His ways. He doesn't expect us to ask Him if we are supposed to spend our 7 day vacation in Italy or France. He wants us to be mature, wise and complete in Him so that we can walk in responsibility and confidence.

Even with more important decisions, God often trusts those who are faithful to Him. He delights Himself in seeing them choose what is right and wise, this wisdom flowing from the communion with Him.

This doesn't mean we don't have to ask God for His leading and advice. He actually likes us to ask for His advice and leading. And as we ask Him for them, He actually leads us to choose what is right, often without having to clearly verbalize what we should do. It is exactly like with a parent on Earth. In the relationship with our earthly father, knowing him makes it obvious what he likes and doesn't like and exempts him from always having to be precise on what to do or not.

Of course, there are times when God clearly verbalizes to us the things He wants us to do. He has His reasons to clearly speak this way in these situations. But many times He simply leads us in making the right decision. In His presence, the Holy Spirit witnesses to our spirit about what is right. Peace generally comes out from this communion, and what we should do appears clearly to us.

The communion with God creates a complicity that makes us acknowledge what the best decision is to please Him in every situation. The communion with Him creates a sensitivity to His joy that helps us see what we are supposed to do.

2- Peace and joy

As we seek God for His leading, His thought comes with peace. He is the Prince of Peace, and when He communicates His thought, it brings peace in us. Peace is a first and important poll to acknowledge God's thought and will.

When we are in His will, we are in perfect peace. Peace doesn't lie. When we seek to know what God's will is in a situation, we need to seek His peace, because He is peace. There is no peace like being in His perfect will.

Some decisions can bring a certain feeling of relief, but not a true peace. In that case, it is often led by a carnal decision that has nothing to do with God's peace. The kind of relief felt then is more a relief of the flesh. It is a temporary relief that is not complete, and it is surrounded with unease, trouble, worry or self-consciousness: all the opposite of what peace is.

God's peace is complete, profound and overwhelming. When we feel it, we clearly know it is God's peace. His peace then is a sure way to know we are in His will, or to know what His will is.

It is the same for joy. God's thoughts always create a joy in us. His thoughts always come with an excitement that is deposited in us. Doing God's will or receiving His thought brings us joy and contentment. This is a second poll to acknowledge God's thought and will.

Joy is a fruit of The Spirit and a witness of His presence and work in us. It is normal to have joy when receiving God's thought or being led into the direction He wants for us. God is joyful, and His Spirit manifests His joy through our communion with Him.

Joy then is another way to acknowledge God's will in a situation.

3- Love

To know God's will in every situation, one essential key is to ask ourselves what love looks like in this situation. We must remember that God is love and His motivation is love; therefore, any of our motivations must be love for whatever we are doing or intend to do. In any situation, we can pursue and manifest love.

4- To walk in all His ways is a sure path

In order to know God's will in a situation, we must make

sure we are walking in all His ways. Some good questions to ask ourselves in the situation would be:

- Am I walking in love in this situation?

- Am I walking in holiness in this situation? (communion with God, purity of the heart, right motivations, peace, love, patience, faithfulness, kindness, etc.)

- Am I walking in righteousness in this situation?

- Am I walking in peace in this situation?

- Am I walking in truth in this situation?

- Am I walking in wisdom in this situation?

- Am I walking in faith in this situation?

If we realize we are actually not walking in one or several of God's ways in this situation, then it can show us how to align our heart to God's heart for the situation. And then the direction to follow will inevitably appear more clearly.

As we have covered, we cannot follow God's ways if we don't follow Him. To walk and remain with Him is what allows us to walk according to Him and like Him. We can walk like Him and be like Him only if we know Him. This is why readjusting our walk in His ways is readjusting our heart toward Him. This heart to heart with Him increases our ability to understand His will, to hear His voice, and to follow His leading.

Psalm 84:5 *"Blessed is the man whose strength is in You; whose heart is set in pilgrimage."*

5- Seek the Kingdom first

Matthew 6:33 *"Seek first the Kingdom of God and His righteousness, and all these things shall be added to you."*

If we seek God's Kingdom first in all situations, then we can be assured that God will take care of us in ALL things. Jesus didn't talk about our primary needs only, but about ALL things. In many situations, the things that we need are not material things. Depending on the situation, our needs may be spiritual, relational, emotional, or circumstantial and can concern us or others involved in the situation. God promises us to intervene in all those areas for our good.

In every situation in which we need to discern God's will, it is good to ask ourselves: "What does it look like to seek the Kingdom of God and His Justice in that situation?" It will help us to see more clearly what we are supposed to do. It will help us to see the situation with God's eyes, and it will make clear which aspects of it need to be treated in priority and according to God. If we choose to do so, then we are guaranteed to be taken care of in all things for our good by God.

Luke 12:31 *"Do not fear little flock, for it is your Father's good pleasure to give you the kingdom."*

God gives us His kingdom. His purpose for us on this earth is to train us to rule with Him in His kingdom. We were made for this from the foundation of the world. When He gave Adam the responsibility of taking care of Eden, He demonstrated to us how much He likes to share His treasures with us and also how much He likes us to rule with Him in His kingdom as sons and heirs of His.

Our role as sons and daughters of God is to operate in the Kingdom as He operates, and the best way to succeed in this is to train ourselves in it, in every situation.

IV- THE PATH OF LIFE

Deuteronomy 30:15-16 *"See, I have set before you today life and good, death and evil, in that I command you today to love The Lord your God, to walk in all His ways, and to keep His commandments, His statutes and His judgments, that you may live and multiply; and The Lord your God will bless you in the land you go to possess."*

Deuteronomy 30:19-20 *"... I have set before you life and death, blessing and cursing ; therefore choose life, that both you and your descendants may live; that you may love The Lord your God, that you may obey His voice, that you may cling to Him, for He is your life and the length of your days; and that you may dwell in the land which The Lord swore to your fathers, to Abraham, Isaac and Jacob, to give them."*

We have seen how walking in each way of God implies a decision. Walking according to each of His ways is a decision. To follow Him and His ways requires a constant submission and agreement with who He is and with His heart.

Therefore, in each situation, we always find ourselves before a choice between two options: to walk according to God's ways or not. This choice is always between good and evil: His spirit or the flesh. It is between life and death.

This is the perpetual choice we have to make, as mentioned in Deuteronomy 30: the choice between life/good and death /evil, between life and death, blessing and cursing.

In each situation, we have the ability to produce life or death, to produce good or evil. According to our decision to walk in the Spirit or in the flesh, we produce the fruits of the path we choose to walk in.

Walking in the Spirit produces life, love, peace, joy, righteousness, and all the good fruits of the Spirit. Walking in the flesh produces destruction, evil, anger, resentment, unforgiveness and all kinds of evil fruits that lead to death.

Jesus is life. If we let Him rule in us, then we bring life around us. We choose the path of life.

In the path of life, we can identify for each way of God some examples of their opposite in the path of death, as follows:

PATH OF LIFE	PATH OF DEATH
Way of righteousness / grace	Self-justification,legalism, unrighteousness,iniquity, unforgiveness
Way of love	Egocentrism,selfishness, indifference, control, fear, rejection, hate, resentment, unforgiveness, bitterness
Way of truth	Fear, control, to believe the voice of the liar, lie, etc.
Way of holiness	Resentment, unforgiveness, anger, bitterness, manifest the flesh, impurity, idolatry, occultism etc.
Way of peace	Argument, quarrel, anger, dissention, division, fear, anxiety, insecurity, control, etc.
Way of wisdom	Unbelief, walk in the flesh, lack of self-control
Way of faith	Impatience, rebellion, unfaithfulness, unbelief.

This can help us realize when we depart from God's heart and ways so that we can readjust our hearts and ways according to His.

As sons and daughters of God, we are called to manifest light, love, life, truth, and justice. In all that we do, in all that we face, in all that is before us, in every situation, we have the opportunity to glorify God and to manifest who He is.

This is all that God's ways are about: manifesting Him. To be like Him.

Lord, we want to know you. And we want to be like you.

About the author

Nassera Victoria is a life-coach and counselor who helps men and women walk in wholeness, and step into their God given destiny.

Visit us at

http://www.mymiracleday.com

www.ingramcontent.com/pod-product-compliance
Lightning Source LLC
LaVergne TN
LVHW051229080426
835513LV00016B/1481